Policy Perspectives: Navigating Public Affairs and Governance

Welcome to "Policy Perspectives: Navigating Public Affairs and Governance." In an increasingly complex and interconnected world, the formulation and implementation of effective public policies play a pivotal role in shaping the present and future of societies. This book serves as a comprehensive guide to the diverse landscape of public affairs and governance, delving into various policy domains that impact our lives on local, national, and global levels. From agriculture and energy to social services and urban planning, this book offers insights into the multifaceted challenges and opportunities faced by policymakers, administrators, researchers, and citizens alike. Join us on a journey through the intricacies of policy-making, examining the factors that influence decisions, the processes involved, and the impacts they have on society. Whether you're a student, professional, or an engaged citizen, "Policy Perspectives" will provide you with a deep understanding of the complex world of public affairs and the importance of effective governance in building sustainable and prosperous communities.

1. Introduction to Public Affairs & Policy
    - The importance of public affairs and policy
    - Overview of key areas and sectors of policy
2. Agriculture & Food Policy

- Agricultural policy and its impact on food production
- Food security and agricultural sustainability
- Government interventions and subsidies in agriculture

3. Energy Policy
- Energy sources and their environmental impacts
- Renewable energy policy and transition to sustainable sources
- Energy conservation and efficiency policies

4. Military Policy
- National defense strategies and military readiness
- Arms control and disarmament policies
- Civil-military relations and defense spending

5. Public Affairs & Administration
- Role of public administration in policy implementation
- Bureaucracy and public service delivery
- Ethics and accountability in public administration

6. Public Policy
- The policy-making process and policy analysis
- Policy evaluation and impact assessment
- Public participation and advocacy in policy development

7. Regional Planning
- Urban and rural development planning
- Infrastructure and transportation planning
- Land use policies and sustainable development

8. Social Policy
- Social welfare programs and safety nets
- Poverty alleviation and social inequality

- Healthcare and education policies

9. Social Security
   - Social security systems and retirement policies
   - Disability benefits and social insurance
   - Challenges and reforms in social security

10. Social Services & Welfare
    - Welfare programs for vulnerable populations
    - Child and family support policies
    - Homelessness and housing policies

11. Urban Planning & Development
    - Urbanization trends and urban planning challenges
    - Smart cities and sustainable urban development
    - Affordable housing and urban infrastructure policies

12. Communication Policy
    - Media regulation and freedom of speech
    - Telecommunications and internet policies
    - Digital divide and access to information

13. Cultural Policy
    - Preservation of cultural heritage and arts
    - Cultural diversity and cultural exchange policies
    - Funding and support for cultural activities

14. Economic Policy
    - Fiscal and monetary policies for economic stability
    - Trade policies and globalization
    - Innovation and economic growth policies

15. Environmental Policy
    - Environmental conservation and natural resource management
    - Climate change mitigation and adaptation policies

The importance of public affairs and policy

Public affairs and policy play a critical role in shaping the social, economic, and political landscape of societies. They encompass the strategies, actions, and decisions taken by governments, organizations, and individuals to address complex challenges, promote public welfare, and facilitate effective governance. Here's an overview of the importance of public affairs and policy:

1. Governance and Decision-Making: Public policy provides the framework for making decisions and governing societies. It establishes rules, regulations, and guidelines that guide the actions of governments, institutions, and individuals. Effective policy formulation and implementation ensure equitable distribution of resources, protection of rights, and the provision of essential services.

2. Social Progress and Development: Sound public policies drive social progress and development by addressing issues such as education, healthcare, poverty, and infrastructure. Policies aimed at improving quality of life, reducing inequalities, and promoting sustainable development contribute to a thriving and equitable society.

3. Economic Stability and Growth: Public policy influences economic stability and growth through measures such as fiscal policies, trade regulations, and investment incentives. Well-designed economic policies can boost employment, attract investment, and promote economic prosperity.

4. Public Health and Safety: Public health policies address health challenges and epidemics, ensuring access to quality healthcare, disease prevention, and emergency preparedness. Policies related to food safety, vaccination, and healthcare access contribute to public well-being.

5. Environmental Protection: Environmental policies play a crucial role in mitigating climate change, conserving natural resources, and preserving biodiversity. Effective policies promote sustainable practices and ensure a healthy environment for present and future generations.

6. Social Justice and Equality: Public affairs and policy initiatives address issues of social justice and equality, ensuring that marginalized and vulnerable populations receive fair treatment, access to opportunities, and protection against discrimination.

7. International Relations: Foreign policy decisions and diplomatic strategies shape a country's interactions with other nations. Effective international policies foster cooperation, resolve conflicts, and address global challenges.

8. Advocacy and Civic Engagement: Public affairs engage citizens in the policy-making process, empowering them to voice concerns, advocate for change, and participate in democratic governance.

9. Regulation and Accountability: Policies establish regulations and standards to ensure ethical conduct, consumer protection, and accountability in various sectors such as finance, healthcare, and technology.

10. Innovation and Research: Public policies often support research and innovation through funding, incentives, and regulations that promote advancements in science, technology, and industry.

11. Crisis Management and Preparedness: Effective public policies provide frameworks for managing crises, such as natural disasters, public health emergencies, and security threats, ensuring timely responses and minimizing negative impacts.

In summary, public affairs and policy are integral to the functioning of societies. They address diverse challenges, promote well-being, and provide a framework for ethical governance. Effective policies not only shape the present but also influence the trajectory of a nation's future by fostering economic growth, social justice, environmental sustainability, and global cooperation.

Overview of key areas and sectors of policy

Policy development and implementation encompass a wide range of key areas and sectors that impact various aspects of society. These areas of policy address diverse challenges, promote social welfare, and guide governance and decision-making. Here's an overview of some key areas and sectors of policy:

1. Economic Policy: Economic policies focus on managing fiscal and monetary measures to ensure economic stability, growth, and equitable distribution of resources. This includes taxation, budgeting, trade regulations, monetary policy, and measures to stimulate employment and investment.

2. Healthcare Policy: Healthcare policies address the organization, delivery, and accessibility of healthcare services. They cover areas such as healthcare financing, insurance, public health initiatives, disease prevention, and regulatory oversight of medical practices and facilities.

3. Education Policy: Education policies govern the structure and standards of educational systems, curriculum development, teacher training, access to education, and measures to improve educational outcomes and promote lifelong learning.

4. Environmental Policy: Environmental policies focus on protecting natural resources, combating climate change, preserving biodiversity, and mitigating pollution. They guide sustainable practices, waste management, and conservation efforts.

5. Social Welfare Policy: Social welfare policies aim to support vulnerable populations, reduce inequality, and address social issues such as poverty, homelessness, and access to social services. They may include social assistance programs, housing policies, and measures to promote social inclusion.

6. Labor and Employment Policy: Labor and employment policies regulate the rights and conditions of workers, including minimum wage laws, workplace safety regulations, labor standards, and policies related to employment discrimination.

7. Housing Policy: Housing policies focus on providing affordable and accessible housing for citizens. They address issues such as housing affordability, rental regulations, housing assistance programs, and urban planning.

8. Criminal Justice Policy: Criminal justice policies cover law enforcement, criminal laws, sentencing guidelines, prison reform, rehabilitation programs, and efforts to promote restorative justice and reduce recidivism.

9. Immigration and Migration Policy: Immigration and migration policies govern the entry, residence, and integration of immigrants and refugees. They address issues related to border control, citizenship, asylum, and multiculturalism.

10. Energy and Resource Policy: Energy and resource policies address the management of energy sources, renewable energy adoption, resource extraction, and measures to reduce dependence on fossil fuels and promote sustainable practices.

11. Foreign Policy and Diplomacy: Foreign policy guides a nation's interactions with other countries. It covers diplomatic relations, international treaties, trade agreements, security alliances, and efforts to address global challenges.

12. Technology and Digital Policy: Technology policies address issues related to internet governance, data privacy, cybersecurity, digital innovation, and the regulation of emerging technologies.

13. Transport and Infrastructure Policy: Transport and infrastructure policies focus on the development of transportation systems, including roadways, public transit, aviation, and infrastructure projects that promote economic development and connectivity.

These are just a few examples of the diverse areas and sectors of policy that governments, organizations, and policymakers address to promote the well-being of citizens, ensure effective governance, and tackle complex societal challenges.

Agricultural policy and its impact on food production

Agricultural policy plays a significant role in shaping food production, distribution, and overall agricultural systems. These policies are implemented by governments to address various challenges and opportunities in the agricultural sector, with the goal of ensuring food security, sustainability, and economic viability. The impact of agricultural policy on food production is profound and can influence factors such as production methods, supply chains, trade, and environmental sustainability. Here's an overview of agricultural policy and its impact on food production:

1. Subsidies and Support Programs: Agricultural policies often include subsidies and financial support for farmers to enhance production, stabilize prices, and ensure a stable food supply. These subsidies can incentivize increased production of specific crops or livestock.

2. Price Control and Market Intervention: Governments may intervene in agricultural markets to stabilize prices and prevent extreme fluctuations. Price controls and market intervention can impact the quantity of food produced and its affordability for consumers.

3. Trade Policies: International trade policies influence the import and export of agricultural products. Trade agreements and tariffs can affect the competitiveness of domestic food production and impact the availability of imported foods.

4. Research and Innovation: Policies that promote agricultural research and innovation lead to the development of advanced farming techniques, improved crop varieties, and more efficient production methods. These advancements contribute to increased food production.

5. Environmental Regulations: Policies focused on environmental sustainability can influence agricultural practices. Regulations related to water usage, pesticide use, and land conservation impact food production methods and their environmental impact.

6. Land Use and Resource Management: Policies that guide land use and resource management impact the types of crops and livestock raised in specific regions. Zoning and land preservation policies affect the availability of agricultural land.

7. Food Safety and Quality Standards: Stringent food safety and quality standards ensure that the food produced meets certain standards for consumer health. These policies impact production practices and processing methods.

8. Agricultural Extension Services: Policies that support agricultural extension services provide farmers with information, training, and technical assistance to improve their production practices and yield.

9. Subsistence vs. Commercial Farming: Policies may influence the balance between subsistence farming for local consumption and commercial farming for export. This affects the variety of crops produced and their availability in the local market.

10. Organic and Sustainable Agriculture: Policies that promote organic and sustainable farming practices impact food production methods by encouraging environmentally friendly approaches that reduce reliance on synthetic inputs.

11. Infrastructure Investment: Investments in rural

infrastructure, such as roads, irrigation systems, and storage facilities, improve farmers' access to markets and impact food production capabilities.

The impact of agricultural policy on food production can be complex and multifaceted. Effective policies consider factors such as food security, economic stability, environmental sustainability, and the well-being of farmers and consumers. Balancing these considerations is crucial to ensuring a resilient and sustainable food production system that meets the needs of a growing global population.

Food security and agricultural sustainability

Food security and agricultural sustainability are closely intertwined concepts that play a crucial role in ensuring a reliable and resilient food supply while safeguarding the environment and natural resources. These concepts address the challenge of providing sufficient, nutritious, and safe food for a growing global population while minimizing the negative impacts of agriculture on ecosystems and future generations. Here's an overview of food security and agricultural sustainability:

Food Security: Food security refers to the availability, access, utilization, and stability of food for all individuals. It encompasses four key dimensions:

1. **Availability:** Ensuring a consistent and adequate supply of food through production, imports, and reserves.
2. **Access:** Ensuring that people have the means to obtain the food they need, including affordability and physical access.
3. **Utilization:** Ensuring that the food consumed meets nutritional requirements and is safe for consumption.
4. **Stability:** Ensuring that the food supply remains stable over time, even in the face of shocks or changes.

Agricultural Sustainability: Agricultural sustainability focuses on producing food in a way that meets present needs without compromising the ability of future generations to meet their own needs. It involves balancing economic, social, and environmental considerations:

1. **Environmental Considerations:** Sustainable agriculture aims to minimize negative impacts on ecosystems, soil health, water resources, and biodiversity. It promotes practices that reduce pollution, conserve natural resources, and mitigate climate change.
2. **Economic Considerations:** Sustainable agricultural systems are economically viable for farmers and communities. They promote fair trade, support local economies, and provide livelihoods for agricultural workers.
3. **Social Considerations:** Sustainable agriculture prioritizes the well-being of farmers, farmworkers, and communities. It ensures equitable access to resources, fair working conditions, and social inclusion.

Interrelationship: Food security and agricultural sustainability are interconnected:

1. **Diverse Food Production:** Sustainable farming practices promote diverse crop varieties and livestock breeds, contributing to food security by reducing reliance on a single food source.
2. **Climate Resilience:** Sustainable agriculture practices enhance the resilience of food systems to climate change, reducing the risk of crop failures and ensuring food availability.
3. **Reduced Food Waste:** Sustainable practices can minimize post-harvest losses and food waste, contributing to improved food availability.
4. **Nutrition:** Sustainable agriculture can improve the quality and nutritional value of food produced, enhancing food security through improved food

utilization.

5. **Long-Term Viability:** By protecting soil fertility, conserving water resources, and avoiding overuse of agrochemicals, sustainable agriculture ensures the long-term viability of food production.

6. **Social Equity:** Promoting fair trade and equitable access to resources supports the economic well-being of farming communities, contributing to food access and affordability.

Addressing food security and promoting agricultural sustainability requires a comprehensive approach that involves governments, farmers, businesses, consumers, and international organizations. By integrating these concepts, societies can create a food system that provides adequate and nutritious food for all while protecting the environment and ensuring the well-being of current and future generations.

Government interventions and subsidies in agriculture

Government interventions and subsidies in agriculture are policy measures implemented by governments to support and influence the agricultural sector. These interventions aim to achieve various objectives, including ensuring food security, promoting rural development, stabilizing agricultural markets, and enhancing the livelihoods of farmers. However, the effectiveness and impacts of these interventions can vary based on the context, the specific policies implemented, and their alignment with broader agricultural and economic goals. Here's an overview of government interventions and subsidies in agriculture:

1. Price Support Programs: Governments may implement price support programs to stabilize agricultural commodity prices. These programs involve setting minimum price levels for certain crops, ensuring that farmers receive a fair price even if market prices are low. Price support can prevent extreme fluctuations and provide income stability for farmers.

2. Subsidies for Inputs: Subsidies for agricultural inputs such as fertilizers, seeds, and irrigation can lower production costs for farmers, improving their profitability and encouraging increased agricultural productivity. These subsidies aim to enhance food production and contribute to food security.

3. Crop Insurance Programs: Crop insurance programs provide financial protection to farmers against crop losses due to factors such as adverse weather conditions, pests, and diseases.

These programs help mitigate risks and provide a safety net for farmers, encouraging them to invest in their agricultural activities.

4. Export Subsidies and Trade Policies: Some governments provide export subsidies to make their agricultural products more competitive in international markets. Trade policies such as tariffs and quotas can influence the flow of agricultural products across borders and protect domestic producers from international competition.

5. Research and Extension Services: Governments may invest in agricultural research, innovation, and extension services to improve farming practices, develop new crop varieties, and enhance productivity. These services provide farmers with valuable information to adopt modern and sustainable farming techniques.

6. Market Information Systems: Governments may establish market information systems that provide farmers with timely and accurate information about market prices, trends, and demand. This information helps farmers make informed decisions and optimize their production and marketing strategies.

7. Rural Development Initiatives: Investments in rural infrastructure, such as roads, storage facilities, and irrigation systems, can improve access to markets and enhance the overall productivity of rural areas. These initiatives contribute to rural development and poverty reduction.

8. Direct Income Support: Some governments provide direct income support to farmers through cash transfers or subsidies, especially during periods of low agricultural income. These programs aim to alleviate poverty among farmers and maintain their livelihoods.

9. Sustainable Agriculture Promotion: Governments may

offer subsidies or incentives to promote sustainable farming practices, organic agriculture, and agroecological methods that reduce environmental impacts and promote long-term agricultural viability.

10. Food Security Programs: Interventions aimed at ensuring food security may include strategic food reserves, distribution of food aid to vulnerable populations, and support for domestic food production to meet national consumption needs.

While government interventions and subsidies can have positive effects on agriculture, they can also have unintended consequences such as distorting market incentives, encouraging overproduction, and increasing dependency on subsidies. Effective policy design, monitoring, and evaluation are essential to balance the benefits and challenges associated with these interventions and ensure that they align with broader agricultural and economic goals.

Energy sources and their environmental impacts

Energy sources play a crucial role in powering modern societies, but they also have varying environmental impacts. The choice of energy sources can significantly influence air quality, greenhouse gas emissions, land use, water consumption, and overall ecological health. Here's an overview of different energy sources and their environmental impacts:

1. Fossil Fuels: Fossil fuels, including coal, oil, and natural gas, have been the primary sources of energy for decades. However, their combustion releases large amounts of carbon dioxide (CO_2), a greenhouse gas that contributes to climate change. Fossil fuel extraction and transportation can also result in environmental damage, including habitat destruction and water pollution.

2. Renewable Energy Sources: Renewable energy sources harness natural processes that replenish themselves, with lower or negligible carbon emissions. However, their environmental impacts can vary:

- **Solar Energy:** Solar power generates electricity by capturing sunlight using photovoltaic cells. It has minimal emissions during operation, but manufacturing solar panels requires energy-intensive processes and certain materials.

- **Wind Energy:** Wind turbines convert wind energy into electricity. Wind power has relatively low emissions and land footprint compared to fossil fuels, but turbine construction can impact local ecosystems and bird populations.

- **Hydropower:** Hydropower generates electricity by harnessing the energy of flowing water. While it produces clean energy, the construction of dams and reservoirs can alter ecosystems, disrupt fish habitats, and displace communities.
- **Geothermal Energy:** Geothermal power utilizes heat from within the Earth for electricity generation. It has minimal emissions and land use impacts, but drilling for geothermal wells can cause localized environmental disruption.

3. Nuclear Energy: Nuclear power generates electricity by nuclear fission. It produces low carbon emissions during operation but poses risks related to nuclear accidents, radioactive waste management, and potential proliferation of nuclear materials.

4. Biomass and Biofuels: Biomass energy utilizes organic materials such as wood, agricultural residues, and biofuels derived from crops for heat and electricity. While it is considered renewable, improper biomass harvesting can lead to deforestation and habitat loss.

5. Natural Gas: Natural gas is a fossil fuel that produces fewer carbon emissions than coal or oil during combustion. However, methane leaks during extraction and transportation can offset these benefits, as methane is a potent greenhouse gas.

6. Coal: Coal is a high-carbon fossil fuel with significant emissions of CO2 and air pollutants when burned. It is associated with air quality degradation, acid rain, and environmental damage from mining.

7. Oil: Oil is a versatile energy source used in transportation, heating, and industrial processes. Its extraction, transportation, and combustion contribute to air pollution, water pollution, and habitat destruction.

8. Environmental Impacts Common to Many Sources: Energy extraction, transportation, and infrastructure development can result in habitat disruption, soil erosion, water pollution, and ecosystem degradation. Additionally, energy production can require significant water resources and contribute to air pollution, affecting human health and ecosystems.

Choosing energy sources with lower environmental impacts is essential for mitigating climate change, reducing pollution, and promoting sustainable development. The transition to cleaner and more sustainable energy sources is a critical step toward minimizing environmental harm and ensuring a healthier planet for current and future generations.

Renewable energy policy and transition to sustainable sources

Renewable energy policy and the transition to sustainable sources are crucial components of efforts to address climate change, reduce pollution, and ensure a more sustainable and resilient energy future. Governments, organizations, and communities around the world are implementing policies and strategies to promote the adoption of renewable energy sources and accelerate the shift away from fossil fuels. Here's an overview of renewable energy policy and the transition to sustainable sources:

1. Renewable Portfolio Standards (RPS) and Mandates: Many governments establish RPS or similar mandates that require a certain percentage of the total energy supply to come from renewable sources by a specific date. These policies create a market demand for renewable energy and drive investments in wind, solar, hydro, and other renewables.

2. Feed-in Tariffs (FiTs) and Power Purchase Agreements (PPAs): Feed-in tariffs and PPAs are mechanisms that provide incentives for renewable energy producers. FiTs guarantee a fixed payment for renewable energy generation, while PPAs involve agreements between producers and consumers (often utilities) to purchase renewable energy at predetermined prices.

3. Tax Incentives and Subsidies: Governments often offer tax incentives, grants, or subsidies to encourage investments in renewable energy projects. These financial incentives can reduce the upfront costs of installations and make renewable energy more attractive to investors.

4. Net Metering and Feed-in Tariff Programs: Net metering allows energy consumers with renewable energy systems (e.g., solar panels) to receive credits for excess energy they generate and feed back into the grid. Feed-in tariff programs offer fixed payments to renewable energy producers for the energy they generate and supply to the grid.

5. Green Procurement and Government Support: Government agencies can lead by example by purchasing renewable energy for their operations. Their commitment to renewable energy sends a signal to the market and encourages private sector adoption.

6. Renewable Energy Certificates (RECs) and Tradable Credits: RECs are tradable certificates that represent the environmental attributes of renewable energy generation. They enable consumers and businesses to support renewable energy even if they can't generate it themselves.

7. Research and Development (R&D) Funding: Investments in R&D support the advancement of renewable energy technologies, making them more efficient, cost-effective, and scalable over time.

8. Infrastructure Development: Policies that facilitate the development of renewable energy infrastructure, such as grid upgrades and energy storage systems, are essential to support the integration of variable renewable sources into the energy mix.

9. Community Engagement and Education: Engaging communities and raising awareness about the benefits of renewable energy can create grassroots support and drive demand for sustainable sources.

10. International Cooperation and Agreements: Global efforts to combat climate change, such as the Paris Agreement, encourage countries to collaborate and set ambitious renewable energy targets.

The transition to sustainable and renewable energy sources requires a comprehensive approach that includes supportive policies, regulatory frameworks, technology development, and public engagement. As renewable technologies become more cost-competitive and efficient, the transition to cleaner energy sources becomes not only environmentally beneficial but also economically viable.

Energy conservation and efficiency policies

Energy conservation and efficiency policies are essential strategies to reduce energy consumption, lower greenhouse gas emissions, and enhance overall energy sustainability. These policies aim to promote the responsible use of energy resources by improving energy efficiency in various sectors and encouraging the adoption of energy-saving technologies and practices. Here's an overview of energy conservation and efficiency policies:

1. **Building Codes and Standards:** Governments establish building codes and standards that require new construction and renovations to meet certain energy efficiency criteria. These codes may include requirements for insulation, lighting, heating, cooling, and appliances.

2. **Energy Efficiency Incentives:** Governments may offer financial incentives, such as rebates, tax credits, or grants, to individuals, businesses, and industries that invest in energy-efficient technologies and practices.

3. **Appliance and Equipment Efficiency Standards:** Regulations that establish minimum energy efficiency standards for appliances, equipment, and vehicles encourage the adoption of more efficient technologies and reduce energy consumption.

4. **Energy Audits and Labeling Programs:** Energy audits assess energy consumption in buildings and recommend measures to improve efficiency. Labeling programs, such as ENERGY STAR, help consumers identify energy-efficient products and buildings.

5. Demand-Side Management Programs: Utilities implement demand-side management programs to encourage customers to reduce energy use during peak demand periods. These programs may include time-of-use pricing, incentives for load shifting, and demand response initiatives.

6. Industrial Efficiency Programs: Industries are often significant energy consumers. Policies targeting industries can include energy audits, benchmarking, and technology upgrades to enhance energy efficiency.

7. Transportation Efficiency Measures: Policies aimed at improving transportation efficiency include promoting public transportation, incentivizing electric and hybrid vehicles, and investing in infrastructure for alternative fuels.

8. Energy Performance Contracts: Energy performance contracts involve third-party providers offering energy efficiency upgrades to buildings and facilities with the guarantee of achieving energy savings. Payments are often based on the realized energy savings.

9. Energy Management Systems: Promoting the adoption of energy management systems in commercial and industrial facilities helps monitor and control energy consumption, leading to better energy efficiency.

10. Education and Outreach: Public awareness campaigns and educational programs help individuals, businesses, and communities understand the importance of energy conservation and efficiency and provide practical tips to save energy.

11. Research and Development: Investments in research and development of new energy-efficient technologies, materials, and practices contribute to ongoing improvements in energy efficiency.

12. Integration with Renewable Energy: Combining energy efficiency measures with renewable energy sources optimizes the overall energy consumption and sustainability of a system.

13. Utility Energy Efficiency Programs: Utilities may offer energy efficiency programs to their customers, providing incentives and resources for energy-saving upgrades and practices.

Energy conservation and efficiency policies play a critical role in achieving energy security, reducing emissions, and addressing climate change. By prioritizing energy efficiency, societies can minimize environmental impact, lower energy costs, and enhance the resilience of energy systems.

National defense strategies and military readiness

National defense strategies and military readiness are crucial components of a country's efforts to protect its sovereignty, security, and interests. These strategies encompass a range of policies, capabilities, and preparations designed to ensure a nation's ability to defend itself against external threats, deter aggression, and respond effectively to security challenges. Here's an overview of national defense strategies and military readiness:

1. National Defense Strategy: A national defense strategy outlines a country's overarching approach to maintaining its security and protecting its interests. It considers geopolitical factors, potential threats, and the nation's defense priorities. This strategy guides the allocation of resources, the development of capabilities, and the establishment of military partnerships.

2. Military Readiness: Military readiness refers to the state of preparedness of a nation's armed forces to respond to a wide range of security scenarios. It involves maintaining a well-trained, well-equipped, and properly organized military force capable of rapidly and effectively deploying and executing missions.

3. Defense Planning and Budgeting: Defense planning involves assessing security risks, identifying potential threats, and allocating resources to build and maintain military capabilities. Budgeting decisions determine the funding allocated to defense programs, including personnel, equipment acquisition, training, and research and development.

4. Force Structure and Modernization: A nation's force structure is the composition and organization of its armed forces, including army, navy, air force, and specialized units. Modernization involves updating and upgrading military equipment, technology, and capabilities to stay current and effective.

5. Deterrence and Prevention: Deterrence aims to discourage potential adversaries from initiating aggression by demonstrating the capability and willingness to respond with overwhelming force. Prevention involves diplomatic efforts, alliances, and partnerships to address security challenges before they escalate into conflict.

6. Intelligence and Reconnaissance: Effective intelligence and reconnaissance capabilities provide critical information about potential threats and adversaries. These capabilities enable decision-makers to assess risks, plan responses, and anticipate developments.

7. Training and Exercises: Military readiness relies on regular training and exercises to maintain the skills and readiness of personnel. Realistic training scenarios help troops prepare for various contingencies and enhance their ability to respond quickly and effectively.

8. Logistical Support: Logistical support ensures that armed forces have the necessary supplies, equipment, and resources to operate in various environments and during extended operations.

9. Cybersecurity and Information Warfare: As technology becomes increasingly integrated into military operations, cybersecurity and information warfare capabilities are essential to protect against cyberattacks, espionage, and disruption of critical systems.

10. Strategic Alliances and Partnerships: Cooperation with allies and partners enhances collective security, intelligence-sharing, and the ability to address shared threats. Military alliances strengthen deterrence and increase the effectiveness of responses.

11. Civil-Military Cooperation: Coordination between the military and civilian agencies is essential for responding to national security challenges, such as natural disasters, pandemics, and humanitarian crises.

12. Flexibility and Adaptability: A well-prepared military force is adaptable and capable of responding to evolving threats and changing circumstances.

National defense strategies and military readiness require careful planning, coordination, and ongoing investment. A strong defense capability contributes to national security, stability, and the protection of a country's interests and values.

Arms control and disarmament policies

Arms control and disarmament policies are initiatives aimed at limiting the proliferation of weapons and reducing the number of weapons in the possession of countries. These policies are designed to enhance global security, prevent conflicts, and promote international stability. Arms control and disarmament efforts seek to reduce the risks associated with the spread of weapons of mass destruction (nuclear, chemical, biological) and conventional weapons. Here's an overview of arms control and disarmament policies:

1. Non-Proliferation Treaties: Non-proliferation treaties are international agreements that aim to prevent the spread of nuclear weapons and other weapons of mass destruction. The Treaty on the Non-Proliferation of Nuclear Weapons (NPT) is a key example, with signatory states committing to disarmament, non-proliferation, and peaceful use of nuclear energy.

2. Arms Control Agreements: Arms control agreements focus on limiting the development, production, and deployment of specific types of weapons. Examples include agreements to limit the number of certain types of conventional weapons, such as the Conventional Forces in Europe (CFE) Treaty.

3. Nuclear Disarmament: Nuclear disarmament seeks to reduce and eventually eliminate nuclear weapons. Countries may engage in bilateral or multilateral negotiations to reduce their nuclear arsenals, enhance transparency, and prevent the use of nuclear weapons.

4. Chemical and Biological Weapons Conventions: The Chemical Weapons Convention (CWC) and the Biological

Weapons Convention (BWC) prohibit the development, production, acquisition, and use of chemical and biological weapons. These treaties aim to prevent the use of these highly destructive and indiscriminate weapons.

5. Arms Trade Treaty: The Arms Trade Treaty (ATT) regulates the international trade in conventional weapons to prevent their diversion to illicit markets or conflict zones where they can exacerbate conflicts and human rights abuses.

6. Confidence-Building Measures: Confidence-building measures aim to reduce tensions and enhance transparency among countries. These measures can include sharing information about military activities, conducting joint military exercises, and promoting open communication channels.

7. Disarmament Verification: Effective disarmament requires verification mechanisms to ensure that countries are complying with their obligations. These mechanisms involve inspections, monitoring, and reporting to confirm the reduction or elimination of weapons.

8. Demilitarization and De-Escalation Zones: Demilitarization and de-escalation zones aim to reduce tensions in specific regions by prohibiting the deployment of certain military forces or weapons. These zones can help prevent conflicts and facilitate diplomatic solutions.

9. Nuclear Arms Control: Nuclear arms control agreements, such as bilateral arms reduction treaties between nuclear-armed states, aim to reduce the number of nuclear weapons and create more stable security environments.

10. Regional Arms Control Initiatives: Regional agreements and initiatives can address specific security challenges in a particular geographic area, promoting stability and cooperation among neighboring countries.

Arms control and disarmament policies play a critical role

in reducing the risk of armed conflicts, preventing the proliferation of dangerous weapons, and fostering international cooperation. However, their effectiveness relies on the commitment of countries to uphold their obligations, engage in negotiations, and work together to build a safer and more secure world.

Civil-military relations and defense spending

Civil-military relations refer to the interaction and dynamic between a country's civilian government and its military forces. These relations are essential for ensuring a balance of power, democratic governance, and effective defense policies. Defense spending is a critical aspect of civil-military relations, as it reflects how a nation allocates resources to its military and how civilian authorities oversee military expenditures. Here's an overview of civil-military relations and defense spending:

1. Civilian Control of the Military: Civilian control of the military is a fundamental principle in democratic societies. It ensures that elected civilian leaders, such as the president or prime minister, have authority over military decision-making. This control helps prevent the military from becoming a separate and independent power center.

2. Defense Policy Formulation: Civilian authorities are responsible for formulating defense policies that align with national security objectives, foreign policy, and budgetary considerations. These policies guide military strategy, force structure, and procurement decisions.

3. Defense Budgeting and Resource Allocation: Civilian authorities determine defense budgets and allocate resources to military programs, operations, equipment acquisition, and personnel. The budgeting process involves weighing national security needs against other spending priorities.

4. Transparency and Accountability: Effective civil-military relations require transparency and accountability in defense spending. Civilian oversight ensures that defense funds are used efficiently and effectively, reducing the risk of corruption and misuse of resources.

5. Legislative Oversight: Legislatures play a crucial role in civil-military relations by overseeing defense policies and budgets. Committees and subcommittees focus on defense matters, scrutinizing spending, procurement decisions, and military operations.

6. Professionalism and Nonpartisanship: Military personnel are expected to remain politically neutral and adhere to civilian control. This nonpartisanship ensures that the military serves the nation as a whole, regardless of political affiliations.

7. Consultation and Decision-Making: Civilian leaders consult with military experts to make informed decisions. While military leaders provide technical expertise, the ultimate decisions are made by elected civilian officials.

8. National Security Strategy: Civilian leaders develop national security strategies that outline the country's security priorities, threats, and responses. The military's role is to execute the strategy within the framework set by civilian authorities.

9. Avoiding Military Intervention in Politics: Maintaining clear boundaries between the military and politics is crucial to prevent military intervention in domestic politics. Civilian leaders must ensure that the military remains subordinate to civilian authority.

10. Military Professionalism: Military professionalism involves adhering to ethical standards, respecting civilian authority, and fulfilling the military's constitutional roles.

Effective civil-military relations contribute to stable governance, democratic norms, and national security. Transparent defense spending and oversight mechanisms ensure that resources are directed toward maintaining a capable and well-equipped military while safeguarding the interests of the civilian population.

Role of public administration in policy implementation

Public administration plays a vital role in the successful implementation of government policies. It involves the management and execution of policies, programs, and projects that have been formulated by elected officials or policymakers. The role of public administration in policy implementation includes various functions and responsibilities:

1. **Planning and Coordination:** Public administrators are responsible for developing detailed plans and strategies to implement policies effectively. This includes identifying goals, objectives, timelines, and resource requirements. They also coordinate efforts among different government agencies and departments involved in the implementation process.

2. **Resource Allocation and Budgeting:** Public administrators allocate resources, including funds, personnel, and equipment, to support policy implementation. They prepare budgets that align with the objectives of the policy and ensure that resources are used efficiently.

3. **Regulation and Compliance:** Administrators develop regulations, guidelines, and standards to ensure that policy implementation is consistent and compliant with laws and regulations. They monitor compliance among government agencies, organizations, and individuals affected by the policy.

4. **Monitoring and Evaluation:** Administrators establish mechanisms to monitor the progress and outcomes of policy

implementation. They collect data, measure performance indicators, and evaluate whether the policy is achieving its intended goals. If necessary, they make adjustments to improve effectiveness.

5. Communication and Public Engagement: Public administrators communicate policy objectives, benefits, and requirements to the public, stakeholders, and affected parties. They seek public input, address concerns, and ensure that there is transparency in the implementation process.

6. Capacity Building: Administrators may identify gaps in knowledge, skills, and resources within the government agencies responsible for policy implementation. They provide training, technical assistance, and capacity-building programs to enhance the capabilities of those involved.

7. Problem Solving and Adaptation: During policy implementation, challenges and unforeseen issues may arise. Administrators are responsible for identifying problems, finding solutions, and adapting strategies to address changing circumstances.

8. Collaboration and Partnerships: Effective policy implementation often requires collaboration with other sectors, including private organizations, non-governmental organizations, and international partners. Administrators establish partnerships to leverage expertise and resources.

9. Feedback Mechanisms: Administrators create mechanisms for feedback and communication between policymakers, implementers, and beneficiaries. This helps identify issues and areas for improvement throughout the implementation process.

10. Accountability and Transparency: Administrators are accountable for the efficient and ethical use of resources during policy implementation. They ensure that decisions are transparent and in line with the public interest.

The role of public administration in policy implementation is crucial for turning policy ideas into tangible actions that deliver positive outcomes for society. Effective administration ensures that policies are executed efficiently, fairly, and in a manner that aligns with the intentions of policymakers while serving the best interests of the public.

Bureaucracy and public service delivery

Bureaucracy plays a significant role in the delivery of public services, as it involves the administrative structure, processes, and personnel responsible for implementing government policies and programs. Public service delivery refers to the provision of essential services, such as healthcare, education, transportation, and social welfare, to the public. The relationship between bureaucracy and public service delivery is crucial for ensuring efficient, effective, and equitable services to citizens. Here's an overview of how bureaucracy impacts public service delivery:

1. Implementation of Policies: Bureaucracy is responsible for translating government policies and decisions into concrete actions. Bureaucrats and civil servants develop plans, allocate resources, and execute programs that deliver services to citizens according to the goals of the policies.

2. Resource Allocation: Bureaucratic agencies allocate resources, including funding, personnel, and infrastructure, to support the delivery of public services. Efficient resource allocation is essential to ensure that services are provided to those who need them most.

3. Program Design and Planning: Bureaucracy plays a role in designing and planning programs that address the specific needs of the population. This includes determining service eligibility criteria, setting objectives, and establishing performance metrics.

4. Monitoring and Evaluation: Bureaucratic agencies are responsible for monitoring the performance of public service delivery programs. This involves tracking progress, assessing outcomes, and making adjustments as needed to improve service quality and effectiveness.

5. Accountability and Transparency: Bureaucracy ensures accountability and transparency in public service delivery. Bureaucratic agencies are accountable to elected officials, policymakers, and the public for the proper use of resources and the achievement of service delivery goals.

6. Efficiency and Effectiveness: Bureaucracy aims to deliver services efficiently and effectively by streamlining processes, reducing bureaucracy, and eliminating unnecessary steps. Efficient public service delivery maximizes the impact of limited resources.

7. Equity and Accessibility: Bureaucracy is responsible for ensuring that public services are accessible to all segments of the population, regardless of socio-economic status, location, or background. This includes addressing disparities and providing services to marginalized communities.

8. Innovation and Adaptation: Bureaucratic agencies are often tasked with identifying innovative approaches to enhance service delivery. They adapt to changing circumstances, emerging technologies, and evolving needs to improve service quality.

9. Communication and Public Engagement: Bureaucracy communicates with the public to inform them about available services, eligibility criteria, and how to access them. Public engagement helps ensure that citizens are aware of the services they can receive.

10. Continuity and Stability: Bureaucratic structures provide continuity and stability in public service delivery, even as political leadership changes. This ensures that essential services continue to be provided regardless of shifts in governance.

The effectiveness of public service delivery depends on the efficiency, transparency, and accountability of the bureaucratic system. Collaborative efforts between bureaucracy, policymakers, civil society, and citizens are essential for improving service quality, addressing challenges, and meeting the diverse needs of the population.

Ethics and accountability in public administration

Ethics and accountability are fundamental principles in public administration that guide the behavior of civil servants, ensure transparency, and promote public trust. Ethical conduct and accountability are essential to maintain the integrity of government institutions and ensure that public resources are used responsibly and effectively. Here's an overview of ethics and accountability in public administration:

Ethics in Public Administration: Ethics in public administration refers to the moral principles and standards that guide the conduct of civil servants in their roles and responsibilities. It involves making decisions and taking actions that prioritize the public interest, uphold integrity, and avoid conflicts of interest. Key aspects of ethics in public administration include:

1. **Integrity:** Civil servants must demonstrate honesty, transparency, and fairness in their actions. They should avoid any form of corruption, bribery, or unethical behavior that undermines the public's trust.
2. **Impartiality:** Public administrators should treat all individuals fairly and without favoritism, regardless of their background, status, or affiliations.
3. **Accountability:** Ethical conduct involves being accountable for one's actions and decisions. Civil servants should take responsibility for their mistakes and take corrective measures.

4. **Conflicts of Interest:** Public administrators should avoid situations where personal interests conflict with their official duties. Transparency and disclosure of potential conflicts are important to maintain public trust.

5. **Confidentiality:** Handling sensitive information with confidentiality is crucial to protect individuals' privacy and maintain the security of government operations.

6. **Service to the Public:** Ethical public administrators prioritize the well-being of citizens and work to provide effective and efficient public services.

Accountability in Public Administration: Accountability refers to the obligation of public administrators to answer for their actions, decisions, and use of resources to elected officials, policymakers, the public, and other stakeholders. It ensures that public servants are responsible for their performance and that they can be held responsible for any failures or misconduct. Key aspects of accountability in public administration include:

1. **Transparency:** Public administrators should be transparent about their actions, decisions, and the use of public resources. Transparency helps prevent corruption and fosters public trust.

2. **Financial Accountability:** Administrators must use public funds responsibly and adhere to budgetary regulations. They should maintain accurate financial records and report on expenditures.

3. **Performance Measurement:** Accountability involves measuring the performance of public programs and services to ensure they achieve their intended outcomes.

4. **Oversight and Evaluation:** Elected officials, legislative bodies, and independent oversight agencies play a role in holding public administrators accountable by conducting audits, evaluations, and investigations.

5. **Legal and Ethical Compliance:** Public administrators must adhere to laws, regulations, and ethical standards in carrying out their responsibilities.
6. **Consequences for Misconduct:** Accountability includes consequences for any misconduct or violations of ethical standards. Disciplinary actions and penalties should be applied when warranted.

Ethics and accountability are intertwined and mutually reinforcing concepts that contribute to effective and responsible public administration. Public administrators who uphold ethical standards and embrace accountability help build public trust, enhance the legitimacy of government institutions, and ensure that public resources are used for the benefit of society.

The policy-making process and policy analysis

The policy-making process is the sequence of steps and activities involved in formulating, adopting, and implementing public policies. Policy analysis is a crucial component of this process, as it involves the systematic examination and evaluation of policy options to inform decision-making. Here's an overview of the policy-making process and policy analysis:

Policy-Making Process: The policy-making process is typically divided into several stages, each of which contributes to the development and implementation of effective policies:

1. **Agenda Setting:** This stage involves identifying issues or problems that require government intervention. Public demand, research, crises, and political priorities can all influence the policy agenda.
2. **Policy Formulation:** In this stage, policymakers and experts develop potential solutions to the identified issues. They analyze available information, gather data, and consider different policy options.
3. **Policy Adoption:** Policymakers decide which policy option to adopt through legislative processes, executive orders, or other decision-making mechanisms.
4. **Policy Implementation:** The adopted policy is put into practice by government agencies and organizations responsible for its execution. Implementation involves planning, resource allocation, and the development of

detailed procedures.

5. **Policy Evaluation:** After implementation, policies are evaluated to determine their effectiveness in achieving the intended goals. Evaluation involves assessing outcomes, impact, and unintended consequences.

6. **Policy Modification or Termination:** Based on evaluation findings, policies may be modified, expanded, scaled back, or terminated. This stage feeds back into the agenda-setting process for potential policy revisions.

Policy Analysis: Policy analysis is a systematic approach to evaluating policy options, predicting their effects, and providing decision-makers with evidence-based recommendations. Key aspects of policy analysis include:

1. **Problem Definition:** Clearly define the problem or issue that the policy aims to address. Identify the causes, scope, and impact of the problem.

2. **Identifying Policy Alternatives:** Generate various policy options that could potentially address the problem. These alternatives should be feasible, practical, and relevant.

3. **Data Collection and Research:** Gather data, evidence, and research relevant to the problem and policy options. This may involve quantitative and qualitative data collection methods.

4. **Impact Assessment:** Analyze the potential impact of each policy option on various stakeholders, the economy, society, and the environment.

5. **Cost-Benefit Analysis:** Evaluate the costs and benefits associated with each policy option. Consider both monetary and non-monetary factors.

6. **Risk Assessment:** Assess the risks and uncertainties associated with each policy option. Consider potential unintended consequences and uncertainties.

7. **Comparative Analysis:** Compare the policy options against each other to identify strengths, weaknesses, opportunities, and threats.

8. **Policy Recommendations:** Based on the analysis, provide policymakers with well-justified recommendations on which policy option is most likely to achieve the desired outcomes.

9. **Communication:** Present the findings and recommendations in a clear and accessible manner, taking into account the needs of policymakers and stakeholders.

10. **Continuous Learning:** Policy analysis involves learning from the outcomes of implemented policies to refine future policy analysis efforts and improve decision-making.

Policy analysis informs policymakers by providing evidence-based insights into the potential outcomes and implications of different policy choices. It helps ensure that policies are well-informed, effective, and aligned with the public interest.

Policy evaluation and impact assessment

Policy evaluation and impact assessment are essential components of the policy-making process. They involve systematic assessments of the outcomes, effectiveness, and unintended consequences of policies to determine their success, inform decision-making, and improve future policies. Here's an overview of policy evaluation and impact assessment:

Policy Evaluation: Policy evaluation is the process of assessing the effectiveness, efficiency, relevance, and sustainability of a policy after it has been implemented. The goal is to determine whether the policy has achieved its intended objectives and to identify any areas for improvement. Key aspects of policy evaluation include:

1. **Outcome Assessment:** Evaluate the actual outcomes and impacts of the policy, considering both intended and unintended consequences. Assess whether the policy has addressed the identified problem or issue.
2. **Effectiveness:** Measure the extent to which the policy has achieved its goals and objectives. Assess whether the desired outcomes have been realized.
3. **Efficiency:** Evaluate the cost-effectiveness of the policy by comparing the resources used with the achieved outcomes. Determine whether the policy has produced the desired results at a reasonable cost.
4. **Relevance:** Assess whether the policy remains relevant given changes in the problem context, societal needs, and technological advancements.
5. **Sustainability:** Evaluate whether the policy's benefits are likely to be sustained over the long term and

whether it can adapt to changing circumstances.

6. **Equity and Distributional Impacts:** Analyze how the policy has affected different segments of the population, considering potential disparities and social equity implications.

7. **Process Evaluation:** Examine the implementation process, including how well the policy was executed, challenges encountered, and lessons learned.

8. **Feedback and Learning:** Use evaluation findings to provide feedback to policymakers, stakeholders, and implementers. Learning from evaluation results can guide the design of future policies.

9. **Decision-Making:** Evaluation results inform decisions about whether the policy should be continued, modified, expanded, or terminated.

Impact Assessment: Impact assessment involves predicting and evaluating the potential effects of a proposed policy before it is implemented. It helps policymakers understand the likely consequences of different policy options and make informed decisions. Key aspects of impact assessment include:

1. **Predicting Outcomes:** Use modeling, simulations, and analysis to predict the potential outcomes of a policy option. Consider economic, social, environmental, and other impacts.

2. **Stakeholder Engagement:** Engage with stakeholders, experts, and the public to gather insights and input on the potential impacts of the proposed policy.

3. **Risk Assessment:** Identify and assess potential risks, uncertainties, and unintended consequences associated with the policy option.

4. **Cost-Benefit Analysis:** Analyze the costs and benefits of the policy option to determine its potential economic impact.

5. **Distributional Analysis:** Consider how the policy

option may affect different groups within the population, including vulnerable and marginalized communities.

6. **Comparative Analysis:** Compare the potential impacts of different policy options to identify the most promising approach.
7. **Policy Design:** Use impact assessment results to refine the design of the policy, address potential negative consequences, and enhance positive outcomes.
8. **Decision-Making:** Impact assessment findings inform decision-makers about the potential effects of different policy options, helping them make informed choices.

Policy evaluation and impact assessment contribute to evidence-based decision-making, ensure accountability, and improve the effectiveness of policies. Together, they enhance the quality of public policies and their impact on society, the economy, and the environment.

Public participation and advocacy in policy development

Public participation and advocacy are integral to the process of policy development and decision-making in democratic societies. They ensure that policies reflect the needs, concerns, and perspectives of the public, enhance transparency, and promote accountability. Here's an overview of the role of public participation and advocacy in policy development:

Public Participation: Public participation involves involving citizens, communities, stakeholders, and civil society organizations in the policy development process. It ensures that policies are informed by diverse viewpoints and that the public has a meaningful role in shaping decisions that affect their lives. Key aspects of public participation include:

1. **Information Sharing:** Provide clear and accessible information about proposed policies, their objectives, potential impacts, and alternatives.
2. **Consultation:** Seek input and feedback from the public, stakeholders, and experts through consultations, surveys, public hearings, and focus groups.
3. **Collaboration:** Encourage collaboration between policymakers, experts, and the public to co-create policies that reflect a wide range of perspectives.
4. **Engagement Strategies:** Employ various engagement strategies, such as online platforms, town hall meetings, workshops, and advisory panels, to reach

different segments of the population.

5. **Inclusion:** Ensure that marginalized and vulnerable groups are included and have a voice in the policy development process.

6. **Feedback Loop:** Provide opportunities for the public to review and provide feedback on draft policies before they are finalized.

7. **Education and Awareness:** Raise awareness and educate the public about policy issues, enabling informed participation.

8. **Transparency:** Communicate how public input influenced policy decisions and demonstrate how public concerns were addressed.

Advocacy: Advocacy involves individuals, groups, and organizations using their influence to promote a specific policy issue, cause, or viewpoint. Advocates aim to shape policies, influence decision-makers, and raise awareness about important matters. Key aspects of advocacy include:

1. **Issue Identification:** Identify issues or causes that require attention and advocate for policy changes to address them.

2. **Building Coalitions:** Form alliances and coalitions with like-minded individuals, organizations, and stakeholders to amplify advocacy efforts.

3. **Messaging and Communication:** Develop persuasive messages and communicate them effectively to policymakers, the public, and the media.

4. **Lobbying:** Engage with policymakers, legislators, and government officials to present arguments, provide evidence, and influence policy decisions.

5. **Mobilization:** Mobilize public support through rallies, campaigns, petitions, and social media to create pressure for policy change.

6. **Policy Research:** Conduct research and gather

evidence to support advocacy positions, making the case for policy change.

7. **Negotiation:** Collaborate with policymakers to find common ground and contribute to policy solutions.
8. **Accountability:** Hold policymakers accountable for their decisions and actions, ensuring they uphold the public interest.

Public participation and advocacy contribute to more inclusive, responsive, and effective policies. They enhance the democratic process by ensuring that policies reflect the diverse needs and aspirations of the public, and they provide opportunities for citizens to engage with their government and make a positive impact on society.

Urban and rural development planning

Urban and rural development planning are processes that aim to guide the growth, infrastructure, and overall improvement of cities, towns, and rural areas. These planning efforts are designed to create sustainable, livable, and well-functioning communities that meet the needs of their residents and promote economic, social, and environmental well-being. Here's an overview of urban and rural development planning:

Urban Development Planning: Urban development planning focuses on managing the growth and development of cities and urban areas. It involves creating policies, strategies, and frameworks to address issues such as population growth, land use, housing, transportation, infrastructure, environmental sustainability, and quality of life. Key aspects of urban development planning include:

1. **Land Use Planning:** Zoning regulations, land allocation, and urban design are used to guide the use of land for residential, commercial, industrial, recreational, and public spaces.
2. **Infrastructure Development:** Planning for transportation, water supply, sewage systems, energy distribution, and other essential infrastructure to support the urban population.
3. **Housing and Affordable Housing:** Developing strategies to ensure access to affordable and quality housing for all residents, including low-income and marginalized communities.
4. **Economic Development:** Promoting job creation, supporting businesses, attracting investments, and

fostering a diverse and sustainable urban economy.

5. **Environmental Sustainability:** Incorporating sustainable practices such as green building, renewable energy, waste management, and green spaces to reduce the environmental impact of urban development.

6. **Community Engagement:** Involving residents, stakeholders, and communities in the planning process to ensure that development aligns with local needs and aspirations.

7. **Transportation and Mobility:** Designing efficient and accessible transportation systems, including public transit, cycling, and pedestrian infrastructure.

8. **Cultural Heritage and Public Spaces:** Preserving cultural heritage sites, creating parks, public spaces, and recreational areas to enhance the urban quality of life.

Rural Development Planning: Rural development planning focuses on improving the economic, social, and environmental conditions of rural areas. It aims to enhance the livelihoods of rural residents, promote sustainable agriculture, and ensure access to essential services. Key aspects of rural development planning include:

1. **Agricultural Diversification:** Encouraging the diversification of rural economies by promoting non-agricultural activities such as agri-tourism, cottage industries, and rural entrepreneurship.

2. **Infrastructure and Basic Services:** Ensuring access to clean water, sanitation, healthcare, education, and other basic services in rural areas.

3. **Agricultural and Livelihood Support:** Developing strategies to improve agricultural productivity, support small farmers, and enhance food security.

4. **Rural Infrastructure:** Building and maintaining

roads, energy supply, telecommunications, and transportation systems to connect rural areas with urban centers.

5. **Natural Resource Management:** Promoting sustainable use of natural resources, conserving biodiversity, and preventing environmental degradation.

6. **Access to Finance:** Providing financial services, microfinance, and credit options to support rural businesses and entrepreneurship.

7. **Social Inclusion:** Ensuring that marginalized and vulnerable communities in rural areas have access to development opportunities and services.

8. **Land Tenure and Property Rights:** Addressing issues related to land ownership, tenure, and access to empower rural communities.

Both urban and rural development planning aim to create balanced, inclusive, and resilient communities. Effective planning requires collaboration among government agencies, local authorities, community members, experts, and stakeholders to ensure that development is sustainable, responsive to local needs, and conducive to the well-being of residents.

Infrastructure and transportation planning

Infrastructure and transportation planning are crucial components of urban and regional development. They involve designing, developing, and maintaining the physical and transportation systems that support economic activities, enhance mobility, and improve the overall quality of life for residents. Here's an overview of infrastructure and transportation planning:

Infrastructure Planning: Infrastructure planning involves the strategic development and management of essential physical systems and facilities that enable a community to function effectively. This includes both social and economic infrastructure. Key aspects of infrastructure planning include:

1. **Transportation Infrastructure:** Planning for roads, highways, bridges, railways, airports, ports, and other transportation networks that connect regions, facilitate movement of goods and people, and support economic growth.
2. **Water and Sanitation Infrastructure:** Ensuring access to clean and safe drinking water, wastewater treatment, and sanitation facilities for residents.
3. **Energy Infrastructure:** Developing energy generation, distribution, and transmission systems to meet the energy needs of the population and businesses.
4. **Communication Infrastructure:** Providing reliable communication networks, including broadband internet and telecommunication services, to facilitate connectivity and information exchange.
5. **Public Health and Education Facilities:** Planning for

healthcare facilities, hospitals, clinics, schools, and educational institutions to meet the needs of the community.

6. **Housing and Urban Amenities:** Developing housing projects, parks, recreational areas, cultural centers, and other amenities that contribute to a high quality of life.

7. **Waste Management and Environmental Infrastructure:** Creating systems for waste collection, recycling, and disposal, as well as environmental management and protection.

8. **Resilience and Sustainability:** Integrating sustainable practices, climate resilience, and disaster preparedness into infrastructure planning to ensure long-term viability.

Transportation Planning: Transportation planning focuses on designing and managing transportation systems that efficiently move people and goods within and between urban and rural areas. It involves considering modes of transportation, traffic management, accessibility, and sustainability. Key aspects of transportation planning include:

1. **Multi-Modal Transportation:** Integrating various transportation modes, including walking, cycling, public transit, and private vehicles, to provide accessible and efficient transportation options.

2. **Traffic Management:** Designing roadways, intersections, and traffic signals to optimize traffic flow, reduce congestion, and enhance safety.

3. **Public Transit Systems:** Planning and expanding public transit networks, such as buses, subways, light rail, and commuter trains, to provide reliable and sustainable transportation options.

4. **Active Transportation:** Creating pedestrian-friendly infrastructure, bike lanes, and pedestrian pathways

to encourage walking and cycling as viable modes of transportation.

5. **Transportation Demand Management:** Implementing strategies to reduce reliance on single-occupancy vehicles, such as carpooling, ride-sharing, and flexible work hours.

6. **Accessibility and Inclusivity:** Ensuring that transportation systems are accessible to people with disabilities and cater to the needs of diverse populations.

7. **Transit-Oriented Development:** Integrating transportation planning with land use planning to promote development around transit hubs and reduce dependency on private vehicles.

8. **Environmental Sustainability:** Incorporating environmentally friendly transportation options, such as electric vehicles, and minimizing the environmental impact of transportation systems.

Effective infrastructure and transportation planning contribute to efficient movement, economic growth, environmental sustainability, and improved quality of life for residents. These planning efforts require collaboration among government agencies, transportation authorities, urban planners, engineers, and community stakeholders to ensure that development is responsive to the needs of the population and the environment.

Land use policies and sustainable development

Land use policies play a critical role in achieving sustainable development by guiding the allocation and management of land for various purposes while minimizing negative environmental, social, and economic impacts. Sustainable development aims to meet the needs of the present without compromising the ability of future generations to meet their own needs. Here's how land use policies contribute to sustainable development:

Balancing Land Use: Land use policies ensure that different land uses, such as residential, commercial, industrial, agricultural, and natural areas, are appropriately located and balanced to promote efficient land utilization.

Conserving Natural Resources: Land use policies help protect natural resources such as forests, wetlands, watersheds, and biodiversity by designating areas for conservation and sustainable use.

Promoting Compact Development: Policies that encourage compact and mixed-use development can reduce urban sprawl, conserve open space, and promote efficient transportation systems.

Preserving Agricultural Land: Land use policies can designate agricultural zones to protect fertile land, ensure food security, and support sustainable farming practices.

Promoting Green Spaces: Policies that require the creation of parks, green belts, and public spaces enhance urban livability, promote physical and mental well-being, and provide recreational opportunities.

Managing Urban Growth: Controlled and planned urban growth through zoning and land use policies prevents overdevelopment, reduces congestion, and maintains the character of communities.

Smart Growth and Transit-Oriented Development: Policies that encourage smart growth and transit-oriented development promote walkability, reduce car dependence, and support public transit, contributing to sustainable transportation systems.

Mixed-Income Housing: Land use policies that promote mixed-income housing contribute to social equity by ensuring diverse communities and reducing the displacement of low-income residents due to gentrification.

Brownfield Redevelopment: Policies that incentivize the redevelopment of brownfield sites (contaminated or abandoned properties) can revitalize urban areas, reduce sprawl, and promote environmental remediation.

Climate Resilience: Land use policies that incorporate climate adaptation strategies, such as floodplain management and green infrastructure, enhance community resilience to climate change impacts.

Stakeholder Engagement: Involving communities, stakeholders, and experts in land use planning ensures that policies are responsive to local needs, aspirations, and concerns.

Integrated Planning: Coordinating land use policies with transportation, environmental, economic, and social policies ensures holistic and integrated approaches to sustainable development.

Monitoring and Evaluation: Regular monitoring and evaluation of land use policies ensure that they are achieving their intended goals and can be adapted as needed.

Effective land use policies require collaboration among

government agencies, urban planners, community groups, developers, and other stakeholders. By promoting responsible and well-planned land use, these policies contribute to sustainable development, improved quality of life, and the preservation of natural resources for future generations.

Social welfare programs and safety nets

Social welfare programs and safety nets are essential components of a well-functioning society, aimed at providing assistance, support, and resources to individuals and families in need. These programs help address poverty, inequality, and social vulnerabilities by ensuring that basic needs are met and promoting economic and social well-being. Here's an overview of social welfare programs and safety nets:

Social Welfare Programs: Social welfare programs encompass a range of initiatives and services that aim to improve the quality of life and well-being of individuals and communities. These programs often target vulnerable and marginalized populations, such as low-income families, children, the elderly, and individuals with disabilities. Some common types of social welfare programs include:

1. **Cash Assistance Programs:** These programs provide financial support to eligible individuals or families in the form of cash transfers. Examples include Temporary Assistance for Needy Families (TANF) and unemployment benefits.
2. **Food Assistance Programs:** Food assistance programs, such as the Supplemental Nutrition Assistance Program (SNAP), provide low-income individuals and families with access to nutritious food.
3. **Housing Assistance:** Housing assistance programs offer affordable housing options for low-income individuals and families, including rental vouchers and subsidized housing.
4. **Healthcare Assistance:** Medicaid and Children's

Health Insurance Program (CHIP) provide low-cost or free healthcare coverage to eligible individuals and families.

5. **Child and Family Services:** Programs like the Child Welfare Services, Child Protective Services, and foster care aim to protect the well-being of children and support families in crisis.

6. **Disability Services:** Disability programs provide support and services to individuals with disabilities to enhance their independence, employment opportunities, and quality of life.

7. **Old Age and Retirement Programs:** Social Security and pension programs provide income support for elderly individuals after retirement.

Safety Nets: Safety nets are social policies and programs designed to provide a cushion for individuals and families facing temporary or unexpected hardships. They act as a safety net to prevent individuals from falling into poverty or experiencing severe economic distress. Safety nets include:

1. **Unemployment Benefits:** These benefits provide financial support to individuals who lose their jobs and are actively seeking new employment.

2. **Emergency Assistance:** Emergency financial assistance is available to individuals facing unexpected crises, such as natural disasters or sudden financial hardships.

3. **Temporary Aid for Needy Families (TANF):** TANF provides temporary financial assistance, job training, and other support services to eligible families.

4. **Disaster Relief Programs:** These programs provide immediate assistance to individuals and communities affected by natural disasters or emergencies.

5. **Homelessness Prevention Programs:** These programs offer support to individuals and families at risk of

homelessness, including rental assistance and case management.

6. **Free and Reduced-Price School Meals:** Schools provide nutritious meals to eligible students from low-income families.

Social welfare programs and safety nets aim to reduce poverty, enhance social equality, and promote the overall well-being of individuals and communities. They play a vital role in addressing systemic inequalities, providing a safety net for those facing challenges, and contributing to a more just and compassionate society.

Poverty alleviation and social inequality

Poverty alleviation and addressing social inequality are crucial goals for societies around the world. Poverty refers to a state of deprivation in which individuals lack access to basic needs such as food, shelter, education, and healthcare. Social inequality refers to disparities in income, wealth, opportunities, and outcomes among different groups within a society. Poverty alleviation and efforts to reduce social inequality are interconnected and involve a range of strategies and interventions. Here's an overview of poverty alleviation and social inequality:

Poverty Alleviation: Poverty alleviation aims to reduce and ultimately eliminate poverty by improving the economic, social, and material well-being of individuals and families. Strategies for poverty alleviation include:

1. **Social Welfare Programs:** Implementing programs that provide financial assistance, food, housing, and healthcare to low-income individuals and families.
2. **Employment Opportunities:** Creating job opportunities, vocational training, and skill development programs to empower individuals to earn a sustainable income.
3. **Education:** Ensuring access to quality education, scholarships, and vocational training to improve skills and employability.
4. **Healthcare Access:** Expanding access to affordable healthcare, including preventive care and medical treatment, to improve overall well-being.
5. **Microfinance and Small Business Support:** Providing

microloans and financial services to low-income individuals to start or expand small businesses.

6. **Agricultural Development:** Supporting sustainable agricultural practices and improving access to markets for smallholder farmers to increase income and food security.

7. **Gender Equality:** Promoting gender equality and women's empowerment, as women often face greater vulnerability to poverty.

8. **Housing and Infrastructure:** Ensuring access to safe and affordable housing, clean water, sanitation, and energy services.

Social Inequality Reduction: Reducing social inequality involves addressing disparities in income, wealth, education, healthcare, and opportunities among different social groups. Strategies for reducing social inequality include:

1. **Progressive Taxation:** Implementing tax policies that place a higher burden on the wealthy to redistribute wealth and fund social programs.

2. **Equal Access to Education:** Providing equal access to quality education, including early childhood education and higher education, to bridge educational gaps.

3. **Healthcare Equity:** Ensuring that all individuals have access to quality healthcare services regardless of their income or social status.

4. **Labor Rights and Minimum Wage:** Enforcing labor rights, fair wages, and safe working conditions to prevent exploitation and improve workers' income.

5. **Affirmative Action:** Implementing policies to provide equal opportunities and address historical disadvantages faced by marginalized groups.

6. **Social Protection Programs:** Expanding social protection programs, such as social security, to

provide a safety net for vulnerable populations.

7. **Land and Property Rights:** Ensuring equitable access to land and property ownership to prevent land concentration and promote economic inclusion.

8. **Promoting Inclusive Economic Growth:** Designing economic policies that prioritize the well-being of all citizens, including measures to reduce income disparities.

9. **Addressing Discrimination:** Addressing discrimination based on race, gender, ethnicity, and other factors that contribute to social inequality.

Efforts to alleviate poverty and reduce social inequality require collaboration among governments, civil society, non-governmental organizations, and the private sector. By implementing comprehensive and sustainable strategies, societies can create more just, equitable, and inclusive environments for all their members.

Healthcare and education policies

Healthcare and education policies are essential components of a country's social and economic development. These policies aim to ensure access to quality healthcare services and education for all citizens, promoting well-being, human capital development, and overall societal progress. Here's an overview of healthcare and education policies:

Healthcare Policies: Healthcare policies focus on providing accessible, affordable, and high-quality healthcare services to individuals and communities. They address a range of issues, including preventive care, medical treatment, public health, and health system management. Key aspects of healthcare policies include:

1. **Universal Healthcare:** Implementing systems that ensure all citizens have access to basic healthcare services regardless of their income or social status.
2. **Health Infrastructure:** Building and maintaining healthcare facilities, hospitals, clinics, and medical centers to provide medical care and services.
3. **Preventive Care:** Promoting preventive measures such as vaccinations, screenings, and health education to reduce the incidence of diseases.
4. **Healthcare Financing:** Developing strategies to fund healthcare services, including government funding, insurance programs, and public-private partnerships.
5. **Primary Care:** Strengthening primary care services to provide essential medical care, disease management, and referrals to specialists.
6. **Quality Standards:** Setting and enforcing quality

standards for medical facilities, healthcare providers, and medical procedures.

7. **Health Promotion:** Encouraging healthy lifestyles and behaviors through public health campaigns and educational initiatives.
8. **Mental Health:** Addressing mental health issues by integrating mental health services into the healthcare system and reducing stigma.

Education Policies: Education policies aim to provide accessible, equitable, and high-quality education to individuals of all ages, fostering human capital development, innovation, and social mobility. Key aspects of education policies include:

1. **Universal Access:** Ensuring equal access to education for all citizens, including marginalized and disadvantaged populations.
2. **Quality Education:** Establishing and maintaining standards for curriculum, teaching methods, and educational materials to ensure quality learning experiences.
3. **Early Childhood Education:** Promoting early childhood education programs to provide a strong foundation for cognitive and social development.
4. **Basic Education:** Ensuring access to primary and secondary education to promote literacy, numeracy, and basic life skills.
5. **Higher Education:** Expanding access to higher education and vocational training to prepare individuals for specialized careers and advanced studies.
6. **Teacher Training:** Providing professional development and training for teachers to enhance their teaching skills and instructional methods.
7. **Equity and Inclusion:** Implementing measures to address gender disparities, promote inclusion of

students with disabilities, and reduce educational inequalities.

8. **Education Funding:** Allocating sufficient resources to education, including government funding, scholarships, and grants.

9. **Technical and Vocational Education:** Offering technical and vocational education and training (TVET) programs to equip students with practical skills for the job market.

Effective healthcare and education policies contribute to human development, economic growth, and social progress. These policies require continuous evaluation, adaptation, and collaboration among government agencies, education and healthcare institutions, communities, and stakeholders to ensure that they remain responsive to evolving needs and challenges.

Social security systems and retirement policies

Social security systems and retirement policies are designed to provide financial support and security to individuals during their retirement years. These policies aim to ensure that people have a reliable source of income after they stop working, promoting financial well-being and reducing the risk of poverty among older adults. Here's an overview of social security systems and retirement policies:

Social Security Systems: Social security systems are government-run programs that provide financial assistance and support to individuals and families in times of need, including retirement. These systems typically encompass a range of benefits and services, including:

1. **Old Age Pensions:** Providing regular payments to individuals who have reached the official retirement age and are no longer in the workforce.
2. **Survivor Benefits:** Offering financial support to the surviving spouses or dependents of deceased individuals who were covered by the social security system.
3. **Disability Benefits:** Providing financial assistance to individuals who are unable to work due to a qualifying disability.
4. **Unemployment Benefits:** Offering temporary financial support to individuals who are unemployed and actively seeking employment.

5. **Healthcare Coverage:** Some social security systems also include healthcare coverage, ensuring access to medical services for retirees and their dependents.

Retirement Policies: Retirement policies encompass a variety of measures aimed at promoting financial security and well-being during the retirement phase of life. These policies address issues such as retirement age, pension eligibility, retirement savings, and post-retirement activities:

1. **Retirement Age:** Governments set a minimum age at which individuals are eligible to receive full retirement benefits. This age can vary based on factors such as life expectancy, labor market conditions, and the sustainability of the social security system.
2. **Pension Eligibility:** Policies determine the criteria individuals must meet to qualify for pension benefits, including years of contributions or service.
3. **Defined Benefit vs. Defined Contribution Plans:** Retirement policies may establish pension plans where benefits are based on a defined formula (defined benefit) or on contributions and investment returns (defined contribution).
4. **Voluntary Retirement Savings:** Encouraging individuals to save for retirement through voluntary retirement accounts, such as individual retirement accounts (IRAs) or employer-sponsored 401(k) plans.
5. **Employer-Sponsored Pensions:** Policies that require or incentivize employers to provide pension plans or retirement benefits to their employees.
6. **Phased Retirement:** Policies that allow individuals to gradually transition from full-time work to retirement, which can be beneficial for both employees and employers.
7. **Post-Retirement Employment:** Addressing policies that allow retirees to work part-time or take on new

roles after retirement without affecting their pension benefits.

8. **Pension Sustainability:** Ensuring the financial sustainability of pension systems by periodically reviewing and adjusting contribution rates, benefits, and retirement age.

Social security systems and retirement policies play a crucial role in ensuring the financial well-being and quality of life of retirees. These policies require careful design, regular monitoring, and adjustments to accommodate changing demographics, economic conditions, and societal needs. By providing a reliable source of income during retirement, these policies contribute to overall social stability and the reduction of poverty among older adults.

Disability benefits and social insurance

Disability benefits and social insurance programs are designed to provide financial assistance and support to individuals who are unable to work due to a qualifying disability. These programs aim to ensure that individuals with disabilities have a source of income to cover their living expenses, medical needs, and other necessities. Here's an overview of disability benefits and social insurance:

Disability Benefits: Disability benefits are financial payments provided to individuals who have a disability that prevents them from engaging in substantial gainful activity or employment. These benefits are intended to help individuals maintain their quality of life and meet their basic needs. Disability benefits typically include:

1. **Cash Payments:** Regular cash payments that provide a portion of the individual's pre-disability income to cover living expenses.
2. **Medical Coverage:** Access to healthcare services and medical coverage to address the specific healthcare needs of individuals with disabilities.
3. **Supplemental Security Income (SSI):** A program in the United States that provides financial assistance to low-income individuals with disabilities, including those who have not worked enough to qualify for Social Security Disability Insurance (SSDI).
4. **Social Security Disability Insurance (SSDI):** A program that provides disability benefits to individuals who have paid Social Security taxes and have earned enough work credits.

5. **Work Incentives:** Some disability benefits programs include work incentives that allow individuals to work part-time or engage in employment without losing their benefits immediately.
6. **Vocational Rehabilitation Services:** Support and services to help individuals with disabilities prepare for, obtain, and maintain employment.

Social Insurance: Social insurance programs are government-run systems that provide financial protection against specific risks or life events, including disability. These programs are funded through contributions from workers, employers, and sometimes the government. Social insurance programs typically cover:

1. **Disability Insurance:** Providing financial benefits to individuals who become disabled and are unable to work due to an injury or illness.
2. **Unemployment Insurance:** Offering temporary financial assistance to individuals who lose their jobs involuntarily.
3. **Pension and Retirement Benefits:** Providing income to retirees based on contributions made during their working years.
4. **Healthcare Coverage:** Some social insurance programs include healthcare coverage, ensuring access to medical services for individuals and their families.
5. **Survivor Benefits:** Offering financial support to the surviving dependents of deceased individuals who were covered by the social insurance program.

Social insurance programs aim to reduce financial vulnerability during times of hardship, ensuring that individuals and families have a safety net to rely on. They contribute to social stability and economic well-being by preventing individuals from falling into poverty due to unexpected events or disabilities.

It's important to note that disability benefit programs and social insurance systems can vary significantly from country to country. The eligibility criteria, benefits structure, funding mechanisms, and administrative processes may differ based on the specific program and the legal and regulatory framework of the country.

Challenges and reforms in social security

Social security systems play a crucial role in providing financial protection and support to individuals during various life stages, including retirement, disability, and unemployment. However, these systems often face challenges due to changing demographics, economic conditions, and societal expectations. Reforms are necessary to ensure the sustainability, effectiveness, and adequacy of social security programs. Here are some challenges and potential reforms in social security:

Challenges:

1. **Aging Population:** As the population ages, there is an increasing number of retirees and a smaller workforce contributing to the system, which can strain funding and resources.
2. **Fiscal Pressures:** Economic downturns, rising healthcare costs, and budget constraints can impact the availability of funds for social security programs.
3. **Longevity:** People are living longer, resulting in longer periods of retirement and increased strain on pension systems.
4. **Workforce Changes:** Changing work patterns, such as the rise of gig work and self-employment, can impact the stability of contributions to social security systems.
5. **Inequality:** Socioeconomic inequalities can lead to disparities in access to social security benefits and contribute to overall societal inequality.
6. **Globalization:** Cross-border migration and labor mobility can complicate the administration of social

security programs and the portability of benefits.

7. **Technological Disruption:** Automation and technological advancements can lead to job displacement and changes in the nature of work, affecting contributions and eligibility.

8. **Mismatch of Benefits:** Benefit structures may not align with modern family structures, leading to challenges for non-traditional families and caregivers.

Reforms:

1. **Adjusting Retirement Age:** Gradually raising the retirement age to reflect increasing life expectancy and promote the sustainability of pension systems.

2. **Diversifying Funding:** Exploring alternative funding mechanisms, such as dedicated taxes or investment earnings, to supplement contributions.

3. **Means-Testing:** Implementing means-testing to ensure that social security benefits are targeted to those who need them the most.

4. **Multi-Pillar Systems:** Adopting multi-pillar systems that combine public, occupational, and private pension options to provide a range of retirement benefits.

5. **Automatic Enrollment:** Implementing automatic enrollment in retirement savings plans to encourage individuals to save for retirement from an early age.

6. **Indexing Benefits:** Indexing benefits to inflation or wage growth to ensure that they keep pace with the cost of living.

7. **Flexible Retirement Options:** Offering flexible retirement options, such as phased retirement or partial pensions, to accommodate varying work preferences.

8. **Long-Term Care Coverage:** Expanding social security coverage to include long-term care benefits to address

the needs of an aging population.

9. **Social Safety Nets:** Strengthening social safety nets to provide assistance to vulnerable populations, including those who may not qualify for traditional social security benefits.

10. **Financial Literacy:** Promoting financial education and literacy to empower individuals to make informed decisions about their retirement and savings.

Reforming social security systems requires careful consideration of societal needs, economic conditions, and long-term sustainability. Policymakers, experts, and stakeholders must collaborate to design reforms that balance the goals of providing adequate benefits, ensuring equity, and securing the financial viability of social security programs.

Welfare programs for vulnerable populations

Welfare programs for vulnerable populations are crucial to providing support, assistance, and opportunities to individuals and groups who face challenges and disadvantages due to various factors such as poverty, disability, age, or discrimination. These programs aim to improve the well-being and quality of life for vulnerable individuals and families by addressing their unique needs and circumstances. Here are some common types of welfare programs for vulnerable populations:

1. **Temporary Assistance for Needy Families (TANF):** TANF provides financial assistance and support to low-income families with children. The program aims to help families achieve self-sufficiency through work activities and job training.

2. **Supplemental Nutrition Assistance Program (SNAP):** SNAP, formerly known as food stamps, provides eligible low-income individuals and families with funds to purchase nutritious food. This program helps reduce food insecurity and improve nutritional outcomes.

3. **Medicaid:** Medicaid is a state and federally funded program that provides health coverage to eligible low-income individuals, including pregnant women, children, elderly individuals, and people with disabilities.

4. **Supplemental Security Income (SSI):** SSI provides financial assistance to low-income individuals who are aged, blind, or

disabled. It helps cover basic living expenses and ensures a minimum level of income.

5. Social Security Disability Insurance (SSDI): SSDI provides financial support to individuals with disabilities who have worked and paid Social Security taxes. It offers benefits to those who are no longer able to work due to their disabilities.

6. Housing Assistance Programs: Various programs, such as Section 8 Housing Choice Vouchers and public housing, provide affordable housing options for low-income individuals and families.

7. Child Care Assistance: Child care assistance programs help low-income families access affordable and high-quality child care services, enabling parents to work or pursue education.

8. Women, Infants, and Children (WIC): WIC offers nutrition education, counseling, and supplemental food to pregnant women, new mothers, and young children to improve their health and well-being.

9. Homelessness Prevention Programs: These programs offer financial assistance, emergency shelter, and support services to individuals and families at risk of homelessness.

10. Elderly Assistance Programs: Programs like Meals on Wheels and senior centers provide services and support to elderly individuals, promoting social engagement and independence.

11. Vocational Rehabilitation Services: These services provide training, education, and support to individuals with disabilities to help them achieve employment and greater independence.

12. Refugee Resettlement Programs: These programs offer support to refugees by providing housing, employment assistance, language classes, and cultural orientation.

13. Foster Care and Adoption Assistance: These programs

support children who are in foster care or adopted by providing financial assistance, case management, and support services.

14. Education Assistance: Scholarships, grants, and tuition assistance programs help low-income individuals access higher education and skills training.

15. Domestic Violence Support: Programs provide assistance, shelter, counseling, and legal support to survivors of domestic violence.

Effective welfare programs for vulnerable populations require coordination among government agencies, community organizations, nonprofits, and stakeholders. These programs help reduce inequalities, alleviate poverty, and create a more inclusive and equitable society by addressing the specific needs and challenges faced by vulnerable individuals and families.

Child and family support policies

Child and family support policies are designed to provide assistance, resources, and services to families to promote the well-being, development, and stability of children and their caregivers. These policies recognize the importance of nurturing a supportive environment for children and ensuring that families have the necessary resources to provide for their children's needs. Here are some common types of child and family support policies:

1. Child Care Subsidies: These programs provide financial assistance to low-income families to help cover the cost of child care services, enabling parents to work or attend school while ensuring quality care for their children.

2. Parental Leave: Paid parental leave policies allow parents to take time off from work to care for a new child without losing their income. These policies promote bonding and support the well-being of both parents and children.

3. Family Medical Leave Act (FMLA): FMLA provides eligible employees with up to 12 weeks of unpaid leave for medical and family reasons, including the birth or adoption of a child, or to care for a seriously ill family member.

4. Child Support Enforcement: These programs help custodial parents receive financial support from non-custodial parents, ensuring that children's basic needs are met.

5. Family Support Centers: These centers offer a range of services, including parenting classes, counseling, and support groups, to help families navigate challenges and build strong relationships.

6. Home Visiting Programs: These programs provide home-based support and guidance to new parents, offering information on child development, parenting skills, and resources for families.

7. Early Childhood Education Programs: Programs like Head Start and Early Head Start offer educational and developmental services to young children from low-income families, preparing them for school success.

8. Family Preservation Services: These services aim to keep families together by providing interventions and support to address issues that could lead to child removal, such as substance abuse or domestic violence.

9. Adoption Assistance: Adoption assistance programs provide financial support, counseling, and resources to families adopting children from foster care or other circumstances.

10. Family Tax Credits: Tax credits such as the Child Tax Credit provide financial relief to families with children, helping to alleviate the costs of raising children.

11. Family Counseling and Mental Health Services: Access to counseling and mental health services can support families in managing stress, conflict, and mental health challenges.

12. Foster Care Support: Foster care policies provide financial assistance, training, and resources to foster parents caring for children in out-of-home placements.

13. School Meals Programs: These programs ensure that children from low-income families have access to nutritious meals during the school day.

14. Housing Assistance: Providing affordable housing options helps families provide stable homes for their children and reduces the risk of homelessness.

15. Child Welfare and Protective Services: These services work to protect children from abuse and neglect by providing support, interventions, and necessary interventions when needed.

Child and family support policies contribute to healthier family dynamics, improved child development outcomes, and reduced poverty and inequality. By addressing the unique needs of families and children, these policies help create a nurturing and supportive environment for the well-being of all family members.

Homelessness and housing policies

Homelessness and housing policies are crucial to addressing the challenges faced by individuals and families without stable housing. These policies aim to prevent homelessness, provide affordable housing options, and support individuals experiencing homelessness in accessing shelter, services, and pathways to permanent housing. Here's an overview of homelessness and housing policies:

1. Homelessness Prevention Programs: These programs offer financial assistance, counseling, and support services to individuals and families at risk of homelessness. They aim to address underlying factors that can lead to homelessness, such as eviction, job loss, or financial instability.

2. Emergency Shelter Services: Emergency shelters provide temporary housing for individuals and families experiencing homelessness. These shelters offer a safe and supportive environment, often including meals, hygiene facilities, and access to social services.

3. Transitional Housing: Transitional housing programs offer temporary housing with supportive services to individuals and families as they transition from homelessness to stable housing. They provide time for participants to address challenges and work toward self-sufficiency.

4. Rapid Re-Housing: Rapid re-housing programs provide short-term financial assistance and support services to help individuals and families quickly move from homelessness to permanent housing. These programs aim to prevent long-term homelessness.

5. Permanent Supportive Housing: Permanent supportive housing combines affordable housing with supportive services for individuals experiencing chronic homelessness or those with disabilities. This approach aims to address both housing and health-related needs.

6. Affordable Housing Development: Policies promoting affordable housing development aim to increase the supply of affordable housing units for low-income individuals and families. These policies may include incentives for developers, zoning changes, and funding for affordable housing projects.

7. Housing Vouchers and Subsidies: Housing vouchers and subsidies provide financial assistance to low-income individuals and families, enabling them to rent housing in the private market. Section 8 Housing Choice Vouchers are an example of such a program.

8. Housing First Approach: The Housing First approach prioritizes providing individuals experiencing homelessness with stable housing as quickly as possible, without requiring them to address other issues such as substance abuse or mental health challenges first.

9. Supportive Services: Supportive services, including case management, mental health counseling, substance abuse treatment, and job training, help individuals experiencing homelessness address underlying challenges and stabilize their lives.

10. Homelessness Counts and Data Collection: Effective policies require accurate data on homelessness. Homelessness counts and data collection efforts help policymakers understand the extent of homelessness, identify trends, and allocate resources effectively.

11. Collaborative Approaches: Addressing homelessness requires collaboration among government agencies, nonprofits, community organizations, and service providers to provide coordinated support and services.

12. Housing Discrimination and Fair Housing Policies: Policies that address housing discrimination and promote fair housing practices ensure that individuals have equal access to housing opportunities regardless of their race, ethnicity, gender, disability, or other characteristics.

13. Tenant Protections: Tenant protections such as rent control, eviction prevention measures, and tenant rights education help safeguard individuals from housing instability.

Effective homelessness and housing policies require a multi-pronged approach that addresses both short-term needs and long-term solutions. By providing stable housing, supportive services, and opportunities for individuals and families, these policies work to reduce homelessness, improve quality of life, and promote social and economic stability.

Urbanization trends and urban planning challenges

Urbanization refers to the increasing concentration of people in urban areas, resulting from rural-to-urban migration and natural population growth. This global trend has led to the growth of cities and the expansion of urban areas. While urbanization can bring economic opportunities and improved living standards, it also presents significant challenges for urban planning and development. Here are some urbanization trends and challenges in urban planning:

Urbanization Trends:

1. **Population Growth:** Cities are experiencing rapid population growth, leading to increased demand for housing, services, and infrastructure.
2. **Rural-to-Urban Migration:** People move from rural areas to cities in search of better job opportunities, education, and improved quality of life.
3. **Megacities and Metropolises:** Some cities are becoming megacities with populations exceeding 10 million, and metropolitan areas are expanding to include interconnected cities and suburbs.
4. **Global Urbanization:** Urbanization is a global phenomenon, with countries across the world experiencing varying rates of urban growth.
5. **Informal Settlements:** Rapid urbanization often leads to the emergence of informal settlements or slums, where people live in inadequate housing without

access to basic services.

Urban Planning Challenges:

1. **Infrastructure Deficits:** Rapid urbanization strains existing infrastructure, including transportation, water supply, sewage systems, and waste management.
2. **Housing Shortages:** As urban populations grow, there's a shortage of affordable housing, leading to informal settlements and homelessness.
3. **Traffic Congestion:** Increased urbanization can result in traffic congestion, pollution, and reduced mobility, affecting the quality of life and economic productivity.
4. **Environmental Degradation:** Urbanization can lead to deforestation, air and water pollution, and loss of green spaces, impacting environmental sustainability.
5. **Resource Constraints:** Urban areas often face challenges in accessing resources like clean water, energy, and food, putting pressure on resource management.
6. **Inequality:** Urbanization can exacerbate income inequality, with disparities in access to education, healthcare, and other services.
7. **Social Cohesion:** Rapid urbanization can strain social cohesion, leading to cultural tensions and challenges in community integration.
8. **Land Use Planning:** Unplanned urban growth can lead to haphazard land use, inefficient land development, and conflicts over land use.
9. **Climate Resilience:** Cities are vulnerable to climate change impacts, such as extreme weather events and rising sea levels, requiring climate-resilient urban planning.
10. **Gentrification:** Gentrification can displace lower-income residents as neighborhoods become more

desirable and property values increase.

Solutions and Approaches:

1. **Comprehensive Urban Planning:** Developing and implementing comprehensive urban plans that address housing, infrastructure, transportation, and environmental sustainability.
2. **Affordable Housing:** Promoting affordable housing initiatives and policies to ensure that housing is accessible to all income groups.
3. **Sustainable Transport:** Encouraging public transportation, cycling, and pedestrian-friendly infrastructure to reduce traffic congestion and pollution.
4. **Green Spaces:** Creating and preserving green spaces within urban areas to improve air quality, provide recreational opportunities, and enhance the urban environment.
5. **Mixed-Use Development:** Designing mixed-use neighborhoods that combine residential, commercial, and recreational spaces to promote vibrant communities.
6. **Social Housing Programs:** Implementing social housing programs to provide safe and affordable housing for low-income residents.
7. **Climate-Resilient Infrastructure:** Designing infrastructure that is resilient to climate change impacts and natural disasters.
8. **Community Engagement:** Involving communities in urban planning decisions to ensure that development meets the needs and aspirations of residents.
9. **Smart City Technologies:** Using technology to enhance urban services, improve efficiency, and promote sustainable urban development.
10. **Data-Driven Decision-Making:** Utilizing data and

analytics to inform urban planning decisions and monitor the effectiveness of policies.

Addressing the challenges of urbanization requires a holistic and collaborative approach involving government, urban planners, community organizations, and residents. By adopting sustainable and inclusive urban planning strategies, cities can manage the impacts of urbanization and create livable, resilient, and vibrant urban environments.

Smart cities and sustainable urban development

Smart cities and sustainable urban development are concepts that aim to create cities that are technologically advanced, environmentally conscious, and socially inclusive. These approaches seek to address the challenges posed by urbanization while promoting efficient resource use, enhancing quality of life, and ensuring long-term environmental and social well-being. Here's an overview of smart cities and sustainable urban development:

Smart Cities:

Smart cities leverage technology and data to enhance urban living, improve services, and optimize resource management. Key characteristics of smart cities include:

1. **Technology Integration:** Smart cities use digital technologies like the Internet of Things (IoT), sensors, data analytics, and artificial intelligence (AI) to gather and analyze data for better decision-making.
2. **Infrastructure Connectivity:** Smart cities integrate various urban systems such as transportation, energy, water supply, waste management, and communication to improve efficiency and user experience.
3. **Sustainable Mobility:** Smart transportation solutions include real-time traffic management, intelligent public transportation, and smart parking systems to reduce congestion and emissions.

4. **Energy Efficiency:** Smart cities focus on energy conservation through smart grids, renewable energy integration, and energy-efficient buildings and lighting.
5. **Waste Management:** Waste collection and disposal are optimized using sensors to monitor fill levels, leading to efficient waste management practices.
6. **Digital Services:** E-governance, online service delivery, and digital platforms connect residents with city services and information.
7. **Data-Driven Decision-Making:** Smart cities use data analytics to make informed decisions about urban planning, service delivery, and resource allocation.

Sustainable Urban Development:

Sustainable urban development prioritizes environmental, economic, and social sustainability to create livable cities for current and future generations. Key principles of sustainable urban development include:

1. **Compact and Mixed-Use Planning:** Designing cities with mixed-use zoning, promoting efficient land use, reducing urban sprawl, and minimizing the need for car-dependent lifestyles.
2. **Green Infrastructure:** Incorporating green spaces, parks, urban gardens, and tree-lined streets to improve air quality, reduce heat islands, and enhance quality of life.
3. **Resource Efficiency:** Using resources efficiently through sustainable building practices, waste reduction, water conservation, and energy-efficient infrastructure.
4. **Renewable Energy Integration:** Incorporating renewable energy sources like solar and wind power to reduce dependence on fossil fuels.
5. **Public Transportation:** Investing in efficient and

accessible public transportation systems to reduce traffic congestion and promote sustainable mobility.

6. **Affordable Housing:** Ensuring access to affordable housing for all residents through inclusive housing policies and mixed-income developments.
7. **Community Engagement:** Engaging residents and stakeholders in urban planning processes to ensure that development meets their needs and aspirations.
8. **Resilience to Climate Change:** Designing cities that are resilient to climate change impacts such as floods, storms, and rising temperatures.
9. **Preservation of Cultural Heritage:** Integrating cultural heritage preservation into urban planning to maintain the city's unique identity and history.

Synergy between Smart Cities and Sustainable Development:

Smart cities and sustainable urban development are interconnected concepts that can complement each other:

1. **Efficiency and Sustainability:** Smart technologies can enhance resource efficiency, leading to more sustainable use of energy, water, and other resources.
2. **Data-Driven Sustainability:** Smart cities use data analytics to monitor environmental indicators, enabling targeted interventions for environmental sustainability.
3. **User-Centric Planning:** Smart cities prioritize residents' needs and preferences, aligning with the goal of creating inclusive and livable urban spaces.
4. **Green Technologies:** Smart cities can integrate renewable energy sources and energy-efficient technologies to promote sustainable urban development.
5. **Citizen Engagement:** Smart city technologies facilitate citizen participation and engagement, empowering residents to contribute to sustainable

development initiatives.

6. **Resilience Planning:** Smart cities can use data to identify vulnerabilities and develop strategies to enhance resilience to climate change and other challenges.
7. **Quality of Life:** Both concepts aim to improve the quality of life for urban residents through enhanced services, connectivity, and a clean environment.

Ultimately, smart cities and sustainable urban development share the common goal of creating cities that are not only technologically advanced but also environmentally and socially sustainable, providing a high quality of life for residents while preserving natural resources and promoting long-term well-being.

Affordable housing and urban infrastructure policies

Affordable housing and urban infrastructure policies are critical components of creating livable and inclusive cities. Affordable housing policies aim to ensure that all residents have access to decent and affordable housing, while urban infrastructure policies focus on developing and maintaining essential urban services and facilities. These policies work together to address housing needs, promote economic growth, and enhance the overall quality of urban life. Here's an overview of both areas:

Affordable Housing Policies:

1. **Subsidized Housing:** Government subsidies and financial incentives are provided to developers to create affordable housing units for low-income individuals and families.
2. **Inclusionary Zoning:** Regulations require developers to include a certain percentage of affordable units in new residential developments.
3. **Rent Control:** Rent control measures limit the amount by which landlords can increase rents in order to protect tenants from excessive rent hikes.
4. **Public Housing:** Government-funded public housing projects provide affordable rental housing to low-income households.
5. **Low-Income Housing Tax Credits:** Tax incentives are offered to developers who build or rehabilitate affordable housing units.

6. **Affordable Housing Trust Funds:** Dedicated funds are established to support the development and preservation of affordable housing.

7. **Housing Vouchers:** Housing Choice Vouchers provide financial assistance to eligible low-income households, allowing them to rent units in the private market.

8. **Community Land Trusts:** Nonprofit organizations acquire and manage land to provide affordable housing options for residents.

Urban Infrastructure Policies:

1. **Transportation Infrastructure:** Policies focus on developing efficient and sustainable transportation systems, including public transit, road networks, and cycling infrastructure.

2. **Water and Sanitation:** Policies ensure access to clean water supply and sanitation services, reducing health risks and improving quality of life.

3. **Energy Infrastructure:** Policies promote the development of efficient and clean energy sources, along with measures to enhance energy conservation.

4. **Waste Management:** Policies aim to manage waste effectively, promoting recycling, composting, and responsible disposal practices.

5. **Green Spaces and Parks:** Policies support the creation and maintenance of green spaces, parks, and recreational facilities for community well-being.

6. **Smart Infrastructure:** Integration of technology and data-driven approaches to manage urban services efficiently and enhance quality of life.

7. **Mixed-Use Development:** Promoting mixed-use zoning encourages the development of neighborhoods where residents can live, work, and access services within close proximity.

8. **Sustainable Building Codes:** Regulations encourage the construction of energy-efficient and environmentally-friendly buildings.

Synergy between Affordable Housing and Urban Infrastructure Policies:

1. **Accessibility:** Well-planned urban infrastructure ensures that affordable housing is connected to essential services, transportation, and employment opportunities.
2. **Affordability:** Access to affordable housing reduces the housing cost burden on residents, allowing them to allocate resources to other needs, including transportation and utilities.
3. **Community Well-Being:** A combination of affordable housing and well-designed urban infrastructure contributes to overall community well-being and quality of life.
4. **Equity:** Both policies promote social equity by ensuring that all residents, regardless of income, have access to basic necessities and services.
5. **Sustainability:** Sustainable urban infrastructure aligns with environmentally-conscious housing development, contributing to resource conservation and reduced environmental impact.
6. **Economic Growth:** Affordable housing and improved urban infrastructure can attract businesses and investment, promoting economic growth and job creation.
7. **Long-Term Planning:** Coordinated policies facilitate comprehensive and long-term urban planning that addresses the needs of all residents.

Balancing affordable housing and urban infrastructure policies is essential for creating cities that are inclusive, resilient, and sustainable. These policies, when implemented in tandem, contribute to the creation of thriving urban environments that prioritize the well-being and dignity of all residents.

Media regulation and freedom of speech

Media regulation and freedom of speech are important and sometimes conflicting aspects of modern society. Media regulation involves the rules, laws, and policies that govern the content and operation of media outlets, while freedom of speech is a fundamental human right that allows individuals to express their thoughts, opinions, and ideas without censorship or restriction. Balancing these two concepts is essential to ensure a healthy and democratic media environment. Here's an overview of media regulation and freedom of speech:

Media Regulation:

1. **Purpose:** Media regulation aims to ensure ethical journalism, protect public interests, prevent misinformation, and maintain social harmony.
2. **Content Standards:** Regulations often set standards for content that is obscene, defamatory, or harmful, in order to protect public morality and individual rights.
3. **Licensing and Ownership:** Governments may require media outlets to obtain licenses to operate, which can influence media ownership and diversity of voices.
4. **Public Interest:** Media regulation often focuses on serving the public interest, ensuring that media outlets provide accurate information, diverse viewpoints, and fair coverage.
5. **Advertising and Commercialization:** Regulations may limit false or misleading advertising, as well as protect vulnerable audiences, such as children, from harmful content.
6. **Media Concentration:** Regulations may aim to prevent

excessive concentration of media ownership, which can lead to limited diversity of voices and viewpoints.

7. **Media Ethics:** Guidelines and standards promote responsible journalism practices, such as fact-checking, unbiased reporting, and respecting individuals' privacy.

Freedom of Speech:

1. **Human Right:** Freedom of speech is enshrined in many international human rights declarations and constitutions as a fundamental right.
2. **Expression of Ideas:** It allows individuals to express their opinions, ideas, beliefs, and criticism of the government or other institutions.
3. **Democratic Society:** Freedom of speech is crucial for an informed citizenry, open debates, and holding governments accountable.
4. **Artistic and Creative Expression:** Freedom of speech includes the right to create and share art, literature, music, and other forms of creative expression.
5. **Protection from Censorship:** It protects individuals from government censorship, allowing a diversity of voices and opinions to be heard.
6. **Limitations:** While freedom of speech is a fundamental right, it may be limited in cases involving hate speech, incitement to violence, or national security concerns.

Balancing Media Regulation and Freedom of Speech:

1. **Protecting Public Interest:** Media regulations can help protect the public from harmful content, misinformation, and incitement while preserving freedom of speech.
2. **Avoiding Censorship:** Regulations should be carefully crafted to avoid suppressing legitimate speech and

stifling dissent.

3. **Transparency:** Clear and transparent regulations can help media outlets understand their responsibilities while respecting freedom of speech.

4. **Independent Oversight:** Independent regulatory bodies can help ensure that media regulations are applied fairly and impartially.

5. **Media Literacy:** Educating the public about media literacy helps individuals critically assess information and navigate the digital landscape.

6. **Adapting to Technology:** Regulations should consider the challenges posed by the digital age, including social media, online platforms, and global reach.

7. **Open Dialogue:** Encouraging open dialogue between regulators, media professionals, and civil society can lead to better-balanced regulations.

The relationship between media regulation and freedom of speech is complex, as both are vital for a functioning democracy. Striking the right balance between the two requires careful consideration of societal needs, ethical principles, and the evolving landscape of media and communication.

Telecommunications and internet policies

Telecommunications and internet policies play a crucial role in shaping the communication landscape, fostering digital inclusion, and ensuring the efficient and fair use of communication technologies. These policies encompass regulations, laws, and guidelines that govern various aspects of telecommunications services and internet usage. They aim to promote competition, protect consumers, enhance connectivity, and uphold principles of open access and innovation. Here's an overview of telecommunications and internet policies:

Telecommunications Policies:

1. **Competition and Market Regulation:** Policies promote fair competition in the telecommunications sector to prevent monopolies and ensure a level playing field for service providers.
2. **Universal Service:** Governments often set goals to ensure that telecommunications services are accessible to all citizens, regardless of location or socioeconomic status.
3. **Infrastructure Sharing:** Encouraging infrastructure sharing among telecom operators can help reduce costs, enhance network coverage, and improve service quality.
4. **Interconnection:** Policies regulate how different telecommunications networks connect and exchange traffic, ensuring seamless communication across networks.
5. **Spectrum Management:** Governments allocate and

manage radio frequency spectrum for various uses, including wireless communication services like mobile and broadband.

6. **Consumer Protection:** Regulations aim to protect consumers from unfair practices, such as misleading advertising, overcharging, and privacy violations.

7. **Digital Inclusion:** Policies work to bridge the digital divide by promoting affordable access to telecommunications services in underserved or rural areas.

8. **Emergency Services:** Regulations require telecom operators to provide emergency services such as 911 or 112 for public safety and immediate assistance.

Internet Policies:

1. **Net Neutrality:** Policies uphold the principle of net neutrality, ensuring that internet service providers treat all data equally and do not discriminate against certain content, applications, or websites.

2. **Data Privacy and Protection:** Regulations govern the collection, storage, and use of personal data by online platforms and service providers to protect user privacy.

3. **Cybersecurity:** Policies aim to safeguard internet infrastructure, systems, and users from cyber threats and attacks through regulations, standards, and incident response mechanisms.

4. **Digital Content Regulation:** Some countries have regulations that govern online content, including hate speech, disinformation, and illegal content, to promote responsible online behavior.

5. **Online Copyright:** Regulations address intellectual property rights and copyright issues in the digital realm, including content sharing and digital distribution.

6. **E-Commerce and Consumer Protection:** Policies cover online transactions, e-commerce regulations, and consumer protection measures to ensure safe and fair online transactions.
7. **Digital Rights:** Policies uphold the rights of individuals to freely express themselves, access information, and participate in online communities.
8. **Broadband Expansion:** Policies focus on expanding broadband access to underserved areas, improving digital connectivity, and promoting high-speed internet availability.

Challenges and Considerations:

1. **Balancing Regulation and Innovation:** Policymakers must strike a balance between regulating the industry for consumer protection and allowing innovation to flourish.
2. **Global vs. National Jurisdiction:** The internet operates globally, raising challenges in harmonizing regulations across jurisdictions while respecting national sovereignty.
3. **Internet Governance:** Policymakers, industry stakeholders, and civil society engage in discussions about internet governance, including issues like data governance and domain name management.
4. **Emerging Technologies:** Rapid technological advancements, such as 5G, artificial intelligence, and the Internet of Things, require adaptable policies to address new challenges and opportunities.
5. **Privacy and Surveillance:** Striking a balance between safeguarding individual privacy and addressing security concerns related to surveillance and data monitoring.
6. **Digital Divide:** Ensuring that policies promote equitable access to telecommunications and the

internet, particularly for marginalized and rural populations.

Telecommunications and internet policies are dynamic and constantly evolving to keep pace with technological advancements and changing societal needs. Effective policies promote digital inclusion, innovation, and responsible use of communication technologies while safeguarding individual rights and public interests.

Digital divide and access to information

The digital divide refers to the gap between individuals and communities that have access to digital technologies, such as the internet and digital devices, and those that do not. This divide can create disparities in accessing information, education, job opportunities, and essential services. Addressing the digital divide is essential for promoting equality, social inclusion, and economic development. Here's an overview of the digital divide and its impact on access to information:

Causes of the Digital Divide:

1. **Infrastructure:** Lack of physical infrastructure, such as broadband internet and reliable electricity, in rural and remote areas can limit access.
2. **Affordability:** High costs of internet services, digital devices, and data plans can hinder access, particularly for low-income individuals and communities.
3. **Digital Literacy:** Lack of digital skills and knowledge to effectively use technology and navigate online resources can be a barrier.
4. **Geographical Disparities:** Urban areas tend to have better access to digital resources compared to rural or underserved areas.
5. **Socioeconomic Factors:** Income inequality, education levels, and employment opportunities can impact access to digital technologies.

Impact on Access to Information:

1. **Educational Opportunities:** The digital divide can

limit students' access to online educational resources, e-learning platforms, and digital libraries.

2. **Information Access:** People with limited access may struggle to access news, health information, government services, and other critical online resources.

3. **Economic Opportunities:** Online job searches, remote work, and e-commerce are increasingly important, and those without internet access miss out on such opportunities.

4. **Civic Engagement:** Access to online government services, voter information, and participation in online discussions can be restricted.

5. **Healthcare:** Lack of access to telemedicine and health information can impact individuals' ability to make informed health decisions.

Addressing the Digital Divide and Improving Access to Information:

1. **Infrastructure Development:** Governments and private sectors can invest in expanding broadband internet coverage to underserved areas.

2. **Affordability Initiatives:** Subsidies, reduced tariffs, and affordable data plans can make internet services more accessible.

3. **Digital Literacy Programs:** Training initiatives can help people develop the skills needed to use digital technologies effectively.

4. **Community Centers:** Establishing community centers with internet access can provide people in underserved areas with a place to connect.

5. **Mobile Connectivity:** Mobile devices and networks can play a significant role in bridging the gap due to their widespread availability.

6. **Public-Private Partnerships:** Collaboration between

governments, non-governmental organizations, and private sectors can drive initiatives to close the digital divide.

7. **Content Localization:** Providing information in local languages can improve access to relevant and meaningful content.
8. **Awareness Campaigns:** Educating communities about the benefits of digital technology and online resources can encourage adoption.
9. **Policy Frameworks:** Governments can enact policies that promote digital inclusion, such as requiring internet service providers to offer affordable plans.
10. **Global Efforts:** International organizations and partnerships can support global initiatives to bridge the digital divide, especially in developing countries.

Addressing the digital divide is essential for ensuring that all individuals have equal opportunities to access information, participate in the digital economy, and engage in civic and educational activities. Closing this divide contributes to a more inclusive and equitable society.

Preservation of cultural heritage and arts

The preservation of cultural heritage and arts is essential for maintaining the identity, history, and traditions of communities and societies. Cultural heritage includes tangible and intangible aspects, such as historic buildings, artifacts, traditions, languages, music, dance, and artistic expressions. Preserving cultural heritage and arts not only connects us to our roots but also enriches our present and future by fostering cultural diversity, creativity, and a sense of belonging. Here's an overview of the importance of preserving cultural heritage and arts:

Cultural Identity and Continuity:

1. **Connecting Generations:** Cultural heritage and arts are bridges that connect present and future generations to their history, ancestors, and cultural identity.
2. **Sense of Belonging:** Preserving heritage fosters a sense of belonging and pride among communities, helping individuals maintain their cultural roots.
3. **Cultural Diversity:** The preservation of various cultural practices and artistic expressions contributes to the diversity and richness of global cultures.

Historical and Educational Value:

1. **Archiving History:** Cultural artifacts, historical sites, and records provide insights into the past, allowing us to understand how societies have evolved.
2. **Educational Resource:** Cultural heritage serves as

a valuable educational resource, teaching us about traditions, social norms, and historical events.

3. **Storytelling:** Cultural heritage and arts often convey stories, myths, and legends that pass down wisdom and lessons from one generation to the next.

Promotion of Creativity and Innovation:

1. **Artistic Inspiration:** Traditional arts and crafts inspire contemporary artists, leading to the development of new artistic forms and expressions.
2. **Innovation from Tradition:** Preserving heritage can inspire innovation by combining traditional knowledge with modern technology and ideas.
3. **Creative Industries:** Cultural heritage contributes to creative industries such as music, literature, performing arts, and crafts, which drive economic growth.

Tourism and Economy:

1. **Cultural Tourism:** Heritage sites, museums, and cultural events attract tourists, contributing to local economies and creating jobs.
2. **Market for Crafts:** Traditional crafts and artworks can be a source of income for artisans and contribute to local economies.

Social Cohesion and Dialogue:

1. **Cultural Exchange:** Sharing cultural heritage fosters understanding, tolerance, and mutual respect among diverse communities.
2. **Fostering Dialogue:** Cultural heritage platforms provide spaces for intercultural dialogue, helping overcome stereotypes and prejudices.

Challenges and Strategies for Preservation:

1. **Environmental Threats:** Natural disasters, climate change, pollution, and urbanization can endanger physical heritage sites and artifacts.
2. **Cultural Erosion:** Rapid globalization and modernization can lead to the loss of traditional practices and languages.
3. **Lack of Funding:** Preservation efforts often require financial resources for conservation, restoration, and awareness campaigns.
4. **Technological Solutions:** Digitization and virtual reality can be used to create digital replicas of heritage sites and artifacts for wider access.
5. **Community Involvement:** Involving local communities in preservation efforts helps ensure that their voices and traditions are respected.
6. **Education and Awareness:** Education programs and public awareness campaigns raise appreciation for cultural heritage and arts.
7. **Legislation and Policies:** Governments can enact laws and policies to protect and preserve cultural heritage sites and artifacts.
8. **International Collaboration:** Collaborative efforts between countries and international organizations can promote cross-border preservation.

Preserving cultural heritage and arts is a shared responsibility that requires collaboration among governments, communities, organizations, and individuals. By valuing and safeguarding our cultural heritage, we can ensure that it continues to enrich our lives and inspire future generations.

Cultural diversity and cultural exchange policies

Cultural diversity and cultural exchange policies are essential for promoting understanding, appreciation, and cooperation among diverse communities and societies. These policies aim to celebrate and respect the variety of cultures, languages, traditions, and perspectives that exist globally. Cultural exchange policies facilitate interactions and collaborations between different cultures, fostering mutual learning and enrichment. Here's an overview of the importance of cultural diversity and cultural exchange policies:

Importance of Cultural Diversity:

1. **Enriching Society:** Cultural diversity adds depth and richness to society, enhancing the quality of life and promoting creative expression.
2. **Preserving Heritage:** Celebrating diverse cultures helps preserve traditional practices, languages, and artistic expressions that might otherwise be lost.
3. **Promoting Tolerance:** Exposure to diverse cultures encourages openness, understanding, and tolerance, reducing stereotypes and prejudices.
4. **Global Interconnectedness:** Cultural diversity reflects the interconnectedness of the world and the shared human experience across different societies.

Benefits of Cultural Exchange:

1. **Cross-Cultural Learning:** Cultural exchange allows

individuals to learn about different traditions, languages, customs, and ways of life.

2. **Mutual Enrichment:** Interaction between cultures leads to the exchange of ideas, knowledge, and artistic influences, enriching all parties involved.

3. **International Relations:** Cultural exchange fosters diplomacy, international cooperation, and peaceful relations between countries.

4. **Personal Growth:** Experiencing different cultures promotes personal growth, empathy, and a broader perspective on global issues.

Cultural Diversity and Exchange Policies:

1. **Cultural Preservation:** Policies focus on protecting and preserving traditional practices, languages, and artistic expressions from cultural erosion.

2. **Multilingualism:** Policies promote the use of multiple languages, recognizing linguistic diversity as a crucial aspect of cultural identity.

3. **Cultural Institutions:** Support for cultural institutions such as museums, galleries, and cultural centers helps promote diversity and preserve heritage.

4. **Promoting Local Arts:** Policies can support local artists and artisans, preserving and promoting their traditional skills and crafts.

5. **International Agreements:** Bilateral and multilateral agreements encourage cultural exchange programs between countries.

6. **Education Programs:** Cultural exchange is often integrated into education programs to expose students to diverse perspectives.

7. **Visa and Immigration Policies:** Facilitating travel for cultural exchange participants encourages international collaboration.

8. **Funding and Grants:** Government grants and funding

support cultural exchange initiatives, festivals, and events.

Challenges and Considerations:

1. **Cultural Sensitivity:** Policies must respect the authenticity and dignity of cultures, avoiding appropriation or distortion.
2. **Inclusivity:** Efforts should include marginalized and underrepresented communities to ensure a fair representation of diverse cultures.
3. **Balancing Modernity and Tradition:** Striking a balance between embracing modernity while preserving cultural heritage can be challenging.
4. **Access and Participation:** Policies should ensure that cultural exchange opportunities are accessible to people from various backgrounds.
5. **Sustainability:** Cultural exchange should have a positive impact on both the hosting and visiting communities, promoting sustainable practices.

Cultural diversity and cultural exchange policies play a vital role in fostering global harmony, mutual respect, and shared understanding. By valuing and promoting cultural diversity, societies can create an inclusive and enriching environment that celebrates the beauty and uniqueness of each culture while promoting a sense of global unity.

Funding and support for cultural activities

Funding and support for cultural activities are essential to promote creativity, preserve cultural heritage, and enrich society. Cultural activities encompass a wide range of artistic expressions, performances, festivals, exhibitions, and heritage preservation efforts that contribute to the vibrancy and diversity of communities. Adequate funding and support ensure that artists, cultural organizations, and heritage projects can thrive and continue to contribute to the cultural fabric of society. Here's an overview of funding and support mechanisms for cultural activities:

Importance of Funding and Support:

1. **Promoting Creativity:** Adequate funding allows artists and creators to pursue their artistic visions and produce innovative cultural works.
2. **Preserving Heritage:** Support for heritage preservation efforts ensures that traditional practices, languages, and historical artifacts are safeguarded.
3. **Community Engagement:** Cultural activities provide platforms for communities to engage, interact, and celebrate their shared heritage.
4. **Economic Impact:** Cultural activities contribute to local economies through tourism, job creation, and the growth of creative industries.

Funding Mechanisms and Support Strategies:

1. **Government Funding:** National, regional, and local governments allocate budgets for cultural programs,

museums, galleries, festivals, and arts organizations.

2. **Grants and Subsidies:** Government agencies, foundations, and arts councils provide grants and subsidies to individual artists and cultural organizations.
3. **Cultural Funds:** Dedicated cultural funds are established to support specific cultural activities, projects, or initiatives.
4. **Corporate Sponsorship:** Private sector companies often sponsor cultural events, performances, and exhibitions as part of their corporate social responsibility initiatives.
5. **Donations and Philanthropy:** Individuals, philanthropic organizations, and patrons of the arts contribute funds to support cultural activities.
6. **Cultural Endowments:** Permanent funds established by governments or foundations generate income to support ongoing cultural activities.
7. **Crowdfunding:** Online crowdfunding platforms allow artists and cultural projects to raise funds directly from the public.
8. **Cultural Organizations:** Non-profit organizations and associations dedicated to cultural activities raise funds through memberships, events, and donations.
9. **Collaborative Funding:** Partnerships between governments, private sector entities, and NGOs pool resources to support larger cultural initiatives.

Support Strategies:

1. **Accessibility:** Ensuring that funding opportunities are accessible to artists and cultural organizations from diverse backgrounds.
2. **Capacity Building:** Offering training, workshops, and mentorship programs to help artists and cultural groups develop their skills and management

capacities.

3. **Cultural Diplomacy:** Governments use cultural activities as a tool for international diplomacy and exchange, promoting their country's culture abroad.
4. **Community Engagement:** Involving local communities in the planning and execution of cultural activities to ensure relevance and ownership.
5. **Public Awareness:** Raising public awareness about the importance of cultural activities and encouraging support from the community.
6. **Evaluation and Impact Assessment:** Regularly assessing the impact of funded cultural activities on audiences, communities, and society.

Challenges and Considerations:

1. **Equity:** Ensuring that funding reaches diverse communities, marginalized artists, and underrepresented cultural forms.
2. **Sustainability:** Establishing long-term funding sources to ensure the continuous support of cultural activities.
3. **Artistic Freedom:** Balancing funding and support with artistic freedom, allowing artists to express themselves without undue influence.
4. **Bureaucracy:** Simplifying application processes and reducing administrative barriers for accessing funds.
5. **Transparency and Accountability:** Ensuring that funds are used transparently and effectively, with proper accountability mechanisms.

Funding and support for cultural activities play a vital role in nurturing creativity, preserving heritage, and fostering cultural exchange. By investing in the arts and cultural sector, societies can create a dynamic and enriching environment that reflects their diverse identities and contributes to their social and economic well-being.

Fiscal and monetary policies for economic stability

Fiscal and monetary policies are two key tools that governments and central banks use to achieve economic stability and growth. These policies influence various aspects of the economy, such as government spending, taxation, money supply, and interest rates. They work together to manage inflation, unemployment, and overall economic activity. Here's an overview of fiscal and monetary policies for economic stability:

Fiscal Policy:

Fiscal policy refers to the use of government spending and taxation to influence the economy. It aims to achieve macroeconomic objectives such as stable economic growth, low unemployment, and controlled inflation.

Expansionary Fiscal Policy: This policy involves increasing government spending and/or reducing taxes to boost aggregate demand and stimulate economic growth. It's typically used during economic downturns to counter recessionary pressures.

Contractionary Fiscal Policy: In contrast, contractionary fiscal policy involves decreasing government spending and/or raising taxes to reduce aggregate demand and control inflation. It's used when the economy is overheating and inflation is a concern.

Automatic Stabilizers: Certain fiscal measures, such as unemployment benefits and progressive income taxes, act as automatic stabilizers. They automatically increase during economic downturns (providing support) and decrease during economic upswings (reducing demand pressures).

Monetary Policy:

Monetary policy involves managing the money supply and interest rates to influence economic activity. Central banks implement monetary policy to achieve price stability and support sustainable economic growth.

Expansionary Monetary Policy: This policy involves reducing interest rates and increasing the money supply to encourage borrowing, investment, and consumer spending. It stimulates economic growth and job creation.

Contractionary Monetary Policy: On the other hand, contractionary monetary policy involves raising interest rates and reducing the money supply to control inflation by slowing down borrowing and spending.

Open Market Operations: Central banks buy or sell government securities in the open market to influence the money supply. Buying securities injects money into the economy, while selling securities withdraws money.

Reserve Requirements: Central banks can require commercial banks to hold a certain amount of reserves against their deposits. Adjusting these requirements can influence the amount of money banks can lend.

Interest Rate Policy: Central banks set short-term interest rates, like the federal funds rate in the U.S. Lowering rates encourages borrowing and spending, while raising rates discourages it.

Coordination and Challenges:

1. **Effective Coordination:** Coordinating fiscal and monetary policies is essential to achieve consistent and balanced economic outcomes.
2. **Time Lags:** Both fiscal and monetary policies have time lags before their impact on the economy is fully

realized, which can complicate decision-making.

3. **Sustainability:** Fiscal policies should be sustainable over the long term to prevent high debt levels that could impact future generations.

4. **Inflation Targeting:** Central banks often set specific inflation targets to guide their monetary policy decisions.

5. **Global Impact:** Global factors, such as exchange rates and international trade, can influence the effectiveness of fiscal and monetary policies.

6. **Unintended Consequences:** Policies can have unintended consequences on different sectors of the economy or specific groups.

Fiscal and monetary policies work together to maintain economic stability by addressing inflation, unemployment, and overall growth. Proper coordination, a clear understanding of economic conditions, and flexible adjustments are essential for effective policy implementation.

Trade policies and globalization

Trade policies and globalization are interconnected concepts that have a significant impact on global economies, businesses, and societies. Trade policies refer to the regulations, agreements, and measures that governments use to manage international trade, while globalization is the process of increasing interconnectedness and interdependence among countries through trade, investment, technology, and cultural exchange. Here's an overview of trade policies and their relationship with globalization:

Trade Policies:

1. **Tariffs:** Tariffs are taxes imposed on imported goods, designed to protect domestic industries and generate revenue for governments.
2. **Non-Tariff Barriers:** These include quotas, licensing requirements, and technical standards that limit the quantity or quality of imported goods.
3. **Trade Agreements:** Bilateral or multilateral agreements establish rules for trade, reduce trade barriers, and promote cooperation among countries.
4. **Free Trade Agreements (FTAs):** FTAs eliminate or reduce tariffs and other trade barriers between member countries to boost trade and economic integration.
5. **World Trade Organization (WTO):** The WTO facilitates global trade negotiations, resolves trade disputes, and enforces trade rules among member countries.
6. **Trade Facilitation:** Policies aimed at simplifying

customs procedures, reducing bureaucratic barriers, and expediting the movement of goods across borders.

Globalization:

1. **Economic Globalization:** The integration of economies through trade, investment, and financial flows, allowing goods, services, capital, and knowledge to move across borders.
2. **Cultural Globalization:** The spread of ideas, values, traditions, and cultural products across countries, facilitated by technology and communication.
3. **Technological Globalization:** The rapid exchange of technological advancements and innovations, shaping industries and transforming economies.
4. **Political Globalization:** The increasing interconnectedness of political and governance systems, leading to international cooperation on issues like climate change and security.

Relationship Between Trade Policies and Globalization:

1. **Promoting Trade:** Trade policies influence the extent to which globalization occurs. Open trade policies foster greater integration and economic interdependence among countries.
2. **Trade Liberalization:** Reducing trade barriers, as seen in free trade agreements, promotes globalization by encouraging cross-border trade and investment.
3. **Global Value Chains:** Globalization has led to the emergence of complex global value chains, where production processes span multiple countries.
4. **Access to Markets:** Trade policies determine the access that businesses have to foreign markets, affecting their ability to reach consumers worldwide.
5. **Competition and Innovation:** Globalization encourages competition, driving businesses to

innovate and improve products and services.

6. **Economic Growth:** Globalization can contribute to economic growth by providing access to new markets, investment opportunities, and technological advancements.

Challenges and Considerations:

1. **Inequality:** Globalization can exacerbate income inequality within and between countries, as benefits are not evenly distributed.
2. **Cultural Homogenization:** Concerns about the loss of cultural diversity due to the spread of dominant global cultures.
3. **Labor and Human Rights:** Globalization can lead to exploitation of labor in countries with weaker labor protections.
4. **Environmental Impact:** Increased trade and production can have environmental consequences, requiring sustainable practices.
5. **Political Implications:** Globalization can influence political dynamics and sovereignty as countries collaborate on global issues.

Trade policies and globalization are complex and multifaceted phenomena that shape economies, societies, and the global landscape. Balancing the benefits of globalization with the challenges it presents requires careful consideration and international cooperation.

Innovation and economic growth policies

Innovation and economic growth policies play a crucial role in fostering technological advancements, boosting productivity, and driving overall economic prosperity. Innovation refers to the development and application of new ideas, processes, products, or services that create value and improve the way we live and work. These policies aim to create an environment that encourages innovation, supports research and development (R&D), and stimulates entrepreneurship. Here's an overview of innovation and economic growth policies:

Importance of Innovation and Economic Growth:

1. **Enhancing Competitiveness:** Innovation drives competitiveness by allowing businesses to offer unique products and services that differentiate them in the market.
2. **Productivity Improvement:** New technologies and processes resulting from innovation increase productivity, leading to higher economic output.
3. **Job Creation:** Innovation-driven industries create jobs, both directly in research and development and indirectly in related sectors.
4. **Solving Challenges:** Innovation addresses societal challenges by developing solutions in areas like healthcare, energy, and the environment.

Innovation and Economic Growth Policies:

1. **Research and Development (R&D) Funding:** Governments allocate funds to support R&D activities

in universities, research institutions, and businesses.

2. **Tax Incentives:** Tax breaks and credits encourage businesses to invest in R&D and innovation.

3. **Intellectual Property Protection:** Strong IP laws protect the rights of innovators, encouraging them to invest in developing new technologies.

4. **Entrepreneurship Support:** Programs that provide funding, mentorship, and networking opportunities for startups and small businesses.

5. **Technology Transfer:** Facilitating the transfer of knowledge and technology from research institutions to commercial applications.

6. **Public-Private Partnerships (PPPs):** Collaboration between the public and private sectors to fund and develop innovative projects.

7. **Education and Skill Development:** Investing in education and training to develop a skilled workforce capable of driving innovation.

8. **Innovation Clusters:** Creating geographic concentrations of companies, research institutions, and support organizations to promote collaboration and knowledge-sharing.

Challenges and Considerations:

1. **Risk and Uncertainty:** Innovation involves risk, as not all ideas result in successful products or services. Policies should encourage experimentation and learning from failure.

2. **Access to Capital:** Ensuring that startups and innovators have access to funding, particularly in early stages when risks are high.

3. **Regulatory Environment:** Policies should strike a balance between promoting innovation and protecting public safety and ethical considerations.

4. **Equitable Distribution:** Efforts should be made to

ensure that the benefits of innovation are shared widely and do not exacerbate inequality.

5. **Long-Term Focus:** Economic growth policies should have a long-term perspective, as the impact of innovation may take time to materialize.

6. **Collaboration and Interdisciplinarity:** Encouraging collaboration across sectors and disciplines can lead to more holistic and impactful innovations.

7. **Sustainability:** Promoting innovation that addresses environmental and social challenges to ensure long-term sustainable growth.

Innovation and economic growth policies are essential for creating an environment that supports creativity, research, and development. By incentivizing and facilitating innovation, governments and organizations can drive economic growth, improve quality of life, and address complex global challenges.

Environmental conservation and natural resource management

Environmental conservation and natural resource management are vital strategies for maintaining the health of ecosystems, preserving biodiversity, and ensuring the sustainable use of natural resources for current and future generations. These efforts aim to address environmental degradation, climate change, and the depletion of natural resources. Here's an overview of environmental conservation and natural resource management:

Environmental Conservation:

1. **Biodiversity Protection:** Conservation efforts focus on protecting and restoring ecosystems to maintain biodiversity, which is essential for ecosystem stability and resilience.
2. **Habitat Restoration:** Restoring degraded habitats, such as forests, wetlands, and coral reefs, helps to recover ecosystems and their services.
3. **Protected Areas:** Establishing and managing protected areas, such as national parks and wildlife reserves, helps preserve biodiversity and unique ecosystems.
4. **Wildlife Conservation:** Protecting endangered species and their habitats through breeding programs, anti-poaching measures, and habitat restoration.
5. **Pollution Control:** Implementing measures to reduce pollution from industries, agriculture, and urban areas

to safeguard air, water, and soil quality.

6. **Climate Change Mitigation:** Conservation plays a role in mitigating climate change by sequestering carbon through reforestation and protecting carbon-rich ecosystems like peatlands.

Natural Resource Management:

1. **Sustainable Agriculture:** Promoting practices that minimize soil erosion, chemical use, and water consumption while enhancing soil health and biodiversity.
2. **Forest Management:** Sustainable logging, afforestation, and reforestation to balance economic benefits with forest preservation.
3. **Water Resource Management:** Managing water resources to ensure availability for current and future generations while protecting aquatic ecosystems.
4. **Fisheries Management:** Implementing quotas, gear restrictions, and marine protected areas to prevent overfishing and maintain fish populations.
5. **Renewable Energy Development:** Promoting the use of renewable energy sources, such as solar, wind, and hydroelectric power, to reduce reliance on fossil fuels.
6. **Waste Management:** Implementing waste reduction, recycling, and waste-to-energy programs to minimize the environmental impact of waste.

Challenges and Considerations:

1. **Interconnectedness:** Ecosystems are interconnected, so actions in one area can have cascading effects on others. Holistic approaches are necessary.
2. **Resource Depletion:** Unsustainable resource extraction can lead to resource depletion, affecting both ecosystems and economies.
3. **Population Growth:** Increasing populations place

additional pressure on natural resources, requiring careful management and sustainable practices.

4. **Climate Change:** Rising temperatures, extreme weather events, and sea-level rise pose challenges to conservation and resource management efforts.

5. **Indigenous Knowledge:** Involving indigenous communities in conservation and resource management can enhance both environmental protection and cultural preservation.

6. **Economic Considerations:** Balancing economic development with environmental conservation can be challenging, but sustainable practices can lead to long-term benefits.

7. **Global Collaboration:** Many environmental challenges are global in nature, requiring international cooperation to address effectively.

Environmental conservation and natural resource management are critical for maintaining the health and sustainability of our planet. Balancing human needs with ecosystem health requires integrated strategies that consider ecological, social, and economic factors to ensure a resilient and thriving future.

Climate change mitigation and adaptation policies

Climate change mitigation and adaptation policies are essential strategies to address the challenges posed by global climate change. Mitigation policies aim to reduce greenhouse gas emissions and slow the pace of climate change, while adaptation policies focus on building resilience and preparing communities for the impacts of climate change that are already occurring. These policies are crucial for safeguarding the planet and ensuring a sustainable future. Here's an overview of climate change mitigation and adaptation policies:

Climate Change Mitigation:

1. **Renewable Energy Promotion:** Policies that encourage the transition from fossil fuels to renewable energy sources like solar, wind, hydro, and geothermal power.
2. **Energy Efficiency:** Implementing measures to reduce energy consumption in buildings, transportation, and industries through technology improvements and behavioral changes.
3. **Carbon Pricing:** Pricing carbon emissions through mechanisms like carbon taxes or cap-and-trade systems to incentivize emission reductions.
4. **Reforestation and Afforestation:** Planting trees and restoring forests to capture carbon dioxide from the atmosphere.
5. **Emission Standards:** Setting strict emission standards for industries and vehicles to limit pollution and

promote cleaner technologies.

6. **Waste Management:** Promoting waste reduction, recycling, and sustainable waste management practices to reduce methane emissions from landfills.

Climate Change Adaptation:

1. **Infrastructure Resilience:** Designing and retrofitting infrastructure to withstand the impacts of climate change, such as stronger storms and rising sea levels.
2. **Water Management:** Developing strategies to manage water resources, prevent water scarcity, and protect against flooding.
3. **Natural Resource Management:** Implementing conservation and restoration efforts to maintain biodiversity and ecosystem services that support resilience.
4. **Urban Planning:** Incorporating climate considerations into urban planning, such as creating green spaces, improving drainage, and enhancing heat resilience.
5. **Disaster Preparedness:** Developing and implementing plans to respond to extreme weather events and other climate-related disasters.
6. **Community Engagement:** Involving local communities in adaptation planning and decision-making to ensure strategies meet their needs.

Challenges and Considerations:

1. **Global Cooperation:** Climate change is a global challenge that requires cooperation among countries to effectively address emissions and adaptation needs.
2. **Equity:** Vulnerable communities often bear the brunt of climate impacts. Policies should address social, economic, and environmental justice.
3. **Long-Term Perspective:** Adaptation policies need to

consider long-term impacts and address challenges that may arise in the future.

4. **Uncertainty:** Climate change impacts can be unpredictable. Adaptation policies should be flexible and capable of adjusting to changing conditions.
5. **Trade-offs:** Some mitigation measures may have unintended consequences. Policies should consider potential trade-offs and unintended impacts.
6. **Technological Innovation:** Harnessing innovation to develop new technologies and approaches for both mitigation and adaptation.
7. **Behavioral Change:** Encouraging individual and collective behavioral changes to reduce emissions and increase resilience.

Mitigation and adaptation policies are critical components of a comprehensive response to climate change. By reducing emissions and preparing for the impacts of a changing climate, societies can better protect their environment, economies, and communities for the future.

Sustainable development and environmental regulations

Sustainable development and environmental regulations are intertwined concepts aimed at achieving economic prosperity, social well-being, and environmental protection for present and future generations. Sustainable development emphasizes the need to balance economic growth with social equity and environmental conservation, while environmental regulations are rules and policies put in place to manage human activities and prevent harm to the environment. Here's an overview of the relationship between sustainable development and environmental regulations:

Sustainable Development:

1. **Triple Bottom Line:** Sustainable development focuses on the "triple bottom line," which considers economic, social, and environmental dimensions of development.
2. **Long-Term Perspective:** It emphasizes meeting current needs without compromising the ability of future generations to meet their needs.
3. **Equity and Social Inclusion:** Sustainable development seeks to ensure that benefits are equitably distributed across society, including marginalized and vulnerable populations.
4. **Resource Efficiency:** It promotes efficient use of resources and reducing waste and pollution through sustainable production and consumption patterns.

5. **Economic Growth:** Economic growth is pursued in ways that are environmentally and socially responsible, considering impacts on natural ecosystems.

Environmental Regulations:

1. **Emission Standards:** Regulations set limits on pollutants emitted by industries, vehicles, and other sources to prevent air and water pollution.
2. **Waste Management:** Regulations govern the handling, treatment, and disposal of hazardous and non-hazardous waste to minimize environmental harm.
3. **Natural Resource Protection:** Regulations protect critical natural resources such as water bodies, forests, and biodiversity from degradation and overexploitation.
4. **Land Use Planning:** Regulations guide land use to prevent urban sprawl, habitat destruction, and inappropriate development.
5. **Ecosystem Conservation:** Regulations establish protected areas, wildlife habitats, and conservation measures to preserve ecosystems and biodiversity.

Relationship Between Sustainable Development and Environmental Regulations:

1. **Balancing Interests:** Environmental regulations help ensure that economic activities align with sustainable development goals by preventing harm to the environment and promoting responsible resource use.
2. **Preventing Tragedy of the Commons:** Regulations prevent overuse and degradation of shared resources, which supports long-term sustainable development.
3. **Incentivizing Innovation:** Regulations can drive innovation by encouraging industries to adopt cleaner

technologies and sustainable practices.

4. **Accountability and Reporting:** Regulations often require businesses to report on their environmental impacts, promoting transparency and accountability in sustainable development efforts.

5. **Policy Integration:** Sustainable development strategies often require integrating environmental regulations with social and economic policies.

6. **Global Commitments:** International agreements, such as the Paris Agreement on climate change, emphasize the need for sustainable development and environmental regulations on a global scale.

Challenges and Considerations:

1. **Complexity:** Balancing economic growth, social equity, and environmental protection can be challenging due to competing priorities.

2. **Implementation:** Effective enforcement and compliance with environmental regulations can be difficult to achieve.

3. **Trade-offs:** Striking the right balance between economic growth and environmental protection may involve trade-offs and challenges.

4. **Global Cooperation:** Many environmental issues are transboundary, requiring international cooperation to address effectively.

5. **Equity Concerns:** Regulations should consider the potential impact on marginalized communities and ensure equitable access to benefits.

Sustainable development and environmental regulations are essential for fostering a harmonious relationship between human activities and the natural world. By aligning economic growth with environmental protection, societies can create a more equitable and prosperous future while safeguarding the planet's resources.

Immigration laws and border control

Immigration laws and border control policies are essential components of a country's governance, shaping the movement of people across borders while addressing security, economic, and humanitarian considerations. Immigration laws regulate the entry, stay, and rights of foreign nationals within a country, while border control measures manage the movement of people and goods at international borders. Here's an overview of immigration laws and border control:

Immigration Laws:

1. **Visa Categories:** Immigration laws establish various visa categories, such as tourist, work, study, and family reunification visas, each with specific eligibility criteria and rights.
2. **Pathways to Citizenship:** Laws outline the requirements and processes for foreign nationals to obtain citizenship, including naturalization.
3. **Admissibility Criteria:** Immigration laws define grounds for inadmissibility, such as criminal history, health issues, or security concerns, which may lead to denial of entry or deportation.
4. **Family Reunification:** Many countries prioritize family reunification, allowing citizens and residents to sponsor family members for immigration.
5. **Humanitarian Protection:** Immigration laws may provide asylum or refuge to individuals fleeing persecution, violence, or conflict in their home countries.
6. **Labor Migration:** Laws regulate the entry of foreign

workers to meet labor market needs while ensuring fair working conditions and preventing exploitation.

Border Control:

1. **Passport and Visa Checks:** Border control officers verify travelers' documents, including passports, visas, and entry permits, to ensure compliance with immigration laws.
2. **Security Screening:** Stringent security checks identify individuals with criminal records or potential security threats.
3. **Customs Inspection:** Officers inspect goods entering or leaving the country to prevent illegal smuggling and enforce trade regulations.
4. **Border Surveillance:** Surveillance technologies, such as cameras, sensors, and drones, aid in monitoring and securing border areas.
5. **Border Crossings:** Control measures include checkpoints, border posts, and international airports where travelers undergo document checks and security screening.
6. **Biometric Identification:** Biometric data, such as fingerprints or facial recognition, may be used to verify the identity of travelers.

Challenges and Considerations:

1. **Security vs. Human Rights:** Striking a balance between national security concerns and protecting the human rights of migrants and refugees can be complex.
2. **Economic Impact:** Immigration policies can influence a country's labor market, economy, and demographic trends.
3. **Humanitarian Concerns:** Effective border control requires consideration of vulnerable populations, such

as asylum seekers and refugees.

4. **Migration Management:** Enforcement of immigration laws and border control requires coordination among various government agencies and international cooperation.
5. **Border Infrastructure:** Adequate border infrastructure is essential for efficient and secure border control.
6. **International Relations:** Immigration and border control policies can affect diplomatic relations and international cooperation.
7. **Public Opinion:** Public attitudes toward immigration and border control policies can influence political decisions and policy changes.

Immigration laws and border control policies are complex and multifaceted, impacting national security, economic prosperity, and humanitarian considerations. Effective policies aim to balance security with human rights while ensuring efficient movement of people and goods across borders.

Refugee and asylum policies

Refugee and asylum policies are critical components of a country's approach to providing protection and support to individuals who have fled their home countries due to persecution, violence, or conflict. These policies address the legal status, rights, and humanitarian assistance for refugees and asylum seekers, with the aim of ensuring their safety and well-being. Here's an overview of refugee and asylum policies:

Refugee and Asylum Definitions:

1. **Refugee:** A refugee is someone who has been forced to flee their home country due to a well-founded fear of persecution based on factors such as race, religion, nationality, political opinion, or membership in a particular social group.
2. **Asylum Seeker:** An asylum seeker is someone who has applied for protection in a foreign country and is awaiting a decision on their application for refugee status.

Refugee and Asylum Policies:

1. **Legal Framework:** Countries establish legal frameworks and procedures for granting refugee status and processing asylum applications in accordance with international conventions, such as the 1951 Refugee Convention.
2. **Asylum Application Process:** Policies outline the process by which individuals can apply for asylum, including submission of evidence and interviews to

assess the validity of their claims.

3. **Non-Refoulement Principle:** Refugee and asylum policies adhere to the principle of non-refoulement, which prohibits the return of individuals to a country where they would face persecution or harm.

4. **Temporary Protection:** Some countries offer temporary protection for individuals who cannot return to their home countries due to conflict or disaster.

5. **Integration and Resettlement:** Policies may outline integration programs and resettlement initiatives to help refugees rebuild their lives in host countries.

6. **Humanitarian Assistance:** Policies address the provision of humanitarian assistance, including shelter, food, healthcare, and education, to refugees and asylum seekers.

Challenges and Considerations:

1. **Humanitarian Concerns:** Policies must balance the humanitarian imperative of providing protection with the challenges of managing large numbers of refugees.

2. **Public Opinion:** Public attitudes toward refugees and asylum seekers can influence policy decisions and support for assistance programs.

3. **Resource Allocation:** Providing support for refugees and asylum seekers requires allocating resources for housing, healthcare, education, and other services.

4. **Integration:** Policies should facilitate the integration of refugees into host societies, enabling them to contribute positively to their new communities.

5. **Backlog and Delays:** Lengthy asylum processing times can leave applicants in limbo and impact their well-being.

6. **Burden Sharing:** International cooperation is essential for distributing the responsibility of hosting and

supporting refugees among countries.

7. **Root Causes:** Addressing the root causes of displacement, such as conflict, violence, and persecution, is essential for long-term solutions.
8. **Vulnerable Groups:** Policies must consider the needs of vulnerable populations, including children, women, the elderly, and people with disabilities.

Refugee and asylum policies reflect a commitment to upholding human rights and providing protection to those in need. Effective policies ensure that refugees and asylum seekers are treated with dignity and respect, while also considering the social, economic, and cultural impacts on host countries.

Integration and multiculturalism policies

Integration and multiculturalism policies are strategies implemented by countries to promote the social cohesion, inclusion, and equal participation of diverse populations, including immigrants and minority groups, within their societies. These policies aim to create an environment where individuals from different cultural backgrounds can contribute to and benefit from their host country while maintaining their cultural identities. Here's an overview of integration and multiculturalism policies:

Integration Policies:

1. **Language Acquisition:** Integration policies often emphasize language learning and proficiency to facilitate communication, education, and employment opportunities.
2. **Education and Skills:** Providing access to quality education and skill development programs helps immigrants and minority groups integrate into the workforce and society.
3. **Employment Opportunities:** Policies that promote equal employment opportunities and combat discrimination help newcomers contribute to the economy and society.
4. **Cultural Understanding:** Encouraging cultural understanding and awareness among host communities and newcomers helps build bridges between different groups.
5. **Social Services:** Access to healthcare, housing, and social services ensures the well-being of all residents,

regardless of their background.

6. **Civic Participation:** Integration policies may encourage immigrants to participate in civic and political activities, fostering a sense of belonging.

Multiculturalism Policies:

1. **Recognition of Diversity:** Multiculturalism policies recognize and value the diversity of cultural, ethnic, and religious backgrounds within society.
2. **Cultural Expression:** These policies promote the right to express and celebrate one's cultural identity without fear of discrimination.
3. **Inclusive Policies:** Multiculturalism policies work to create inclusive environments where cultural differences are respected and celebrated.
4. **Cultural Institutions:** Supporting cultural institutions, festivals, and events that showcase diverse cultures promotes cross-cultural understanding.
5. **Media and Representation:** Encouraging diverse representation in media and public spaces helps combat stereotypes and fosters a more inclusive society.
6. **Anti-Discrimination Measures:** Multiculturalism policies include measures to combat discrimination and promote equal treatment for all.

Challenges and Considerations:

1. **Balancing Identities:** Integrating while maintaining one's cultural identity can be complex, requiring a delicate balance.
2. **Social Cohesion:** Striking a balance between cultural diversity and social cohesion is a challenge that requires ongoing efforts.
3. **Political Debate:** Multiculturalism policies can be the

subject of political debate and criticism, with differing opinions on their effectiveness.

4. **Segregation:** Fostering integration can be challenging if certain communities become isolated due to linguistic, cultural, or economic factors.
5. **Changing Attitudes:** Changing attitudes and fostering cross-cultural understanding require time, education, and community engagement.
6. **Equitable Access:** Ensuring that all groups have equitable access to opportunities is crucial for successful integration.

Integration and multiculturalism policies play a vital role in creating diverse and inclusive societies. When effectively implemented, these policies can lead to social harmony, economic prosperity, and a shared sense of belonging among all residents.

Role of international organizations in global governance

International organizations play a significant role in global governance by facilitating cooperation, coordination, and the management of international issues and challenges. These organizations bring together countries, non-governmental organizations (NGOs), and other stakeholders to address global problems that transcend national boundaries. Their role ranges from promoting peace and security to addressing economic, environmental, social, and humanitarian concerns. Here's an overview of the role of international organizations in global governance:

1. Peace and Security:

- The United Nations (UN) and its Security Council work to prevent conflicts, facilitate peace negotiations, and maintain international security through diplomatic efforts, sanctions, and peacekeeping missions.

2. Human Rights and Humanitarian Affairs:

- International organizations such as the UN Human Rights Council and the International Committee of the Red Cross (ICRC) promote human rights, humanitarian law, and provide aid during crises.

3. Economic Cooperation:

- Organizations like the World Trade Organization (WTO), International Monetary Fund (IMF), and World

Bank facilitate global economic cooperation, trade negotiations, financial stability, and development funding.

4. Environmental Protection:

- The United Nations Environment Programme (UNEP) and other organizations address environmental challenges such as climate change, pollution, and conservation through international agreements and initiatives.

5. Health and Pandemic Response:

- The World Health Organization (WHO) coordinates global health efforts, monitors disease outbreaks, and provides guidance during health emergencies, such as pandemics.

6. Development and Poverty Alleviation:

- Organizations like the United Nations Development Programme (UNDP) work to reduce poverty, promote sustainable development, and address inequalities across countries.

7. Humanitarian Assistance:

- Organizations like the United Nations High Commissioner for Refugees (UNHCR) provide aid and support to refugees, internally displaced persons, and victims of conflicts and disasters.

8. Cultural Exchange and Education:

- The United Nations Educational, Scientific and Cultural Organization (UNESCO) promotes cultural diversity, education, and scientific cooperation to foster mutual understanding.

9. Rule of Law and Justice:

- International organizations like the International Court of Justice (ICJ) settle disputes between states and uphold international law.

10. Conflict Resolution and Mediation:

- Organizations such as the Organization for Security and Co-operation in Europe (OSCE) engage in conflict resolution, mediation, and building trust among member states.

11. Norms and Standards:

- International organizations set norms, standards, and guidelines in various fields, from aviation (International Civil Aviation Organization) to telecommunications (International Telecommunication Union).

Challenges and Considerations:

1. **Sovereignty:** Balancing international cooperation with the sovereignty of member states can be a challenge.
2. **Funding:** International organizations often rely on member states' contributions, leading to potential financial constraints.
3. **Representation:** Ensuring equitable representation and decision-making among member states can be complex.
4. **Effectiveness:** The effectiveness of international organizations can vary due to differences in resources, mandates, and political dynamics.
5. **Coordination:** Coordinating efforts among various international organizations can sometimes be challenging.

6. **Accountability:** Ensuring accountability and transparency in decision-making and operations is essential.

International organizations provide platforms for countries to collaborate on global challenges, foster diplomatic relations, and work toward shared goals. Their role in global governance contributes to promoting peace, security, development, and cooperation in an interconnected world.

United Nations and specialized agencies

The United Nations (UN) is an international organization founded in 1945 to promote peace, security, cooperation, and development among nations. It consists of various specialized agencies, programs, and bodies that address specific issues and challenges in a coordinated manner. These specialized agencies operate within the framework of the UN but have their own governance structures and mandates. Here are some of the key specialized agencies and programs under the United Nations:

1. World Health Organization (WHO):

- Mandate: Responsible for international public health, disease prevention, health emergencies, and promoting global health standards.

2. United Nations Educational, Scientific and Cultural Organization (UNESCO):

- Mandate: Promotes education, cultural exchange, scientific research, and preservation of cultural heritage.

3. International Monetary Fund (IMF):

- Mandate: Facilitates international monetary cooperation, exchange rate stability, balanced trade, and financial stability.

4. World Bank Group:

- Mandate: Provides financial and technical assistance for development projects in areas such as poverty reduction, infrastructure, and healthcare.

5. International Labour Organization (ILO):

- Mandate: Sets labor standards, promotes decent work, and addresses issues related to employment, social protection, and workers' rights.

6. United Nations Children's Fund (UNICEF):

- Mandate: Focuses on child survival, development, education, and protection, particularly for vulnerable and disadvantaged children.

7. Food and Agriculture Organization (FAO):

- Mandate: Works to eliminate hunger, promote sustainable agriculture, and improve food security and nutrition.

8. World Food Programme (WFP):

- Mandate: Addresses hunger and malnutrition by providing food assistance during emergencies and supporting development programs.

9. United Nations High Commissioner for Refugees (UNHCR):

- Mandate: Protects and assists refugees and internally displaced persons, providing shelter, aid, and support.

10. United Nations Environment Programme (UNEP):

- Mandate: Coordinates global efforts to address environmental challenges, including climate change, pollution, and biodiversity loss.

11. International Atomic Energy Agency (IAEA):

- Mandate: Promotes the peaceful use of nuclear energy, safeguards against nuclear proliferation, and supports nuclear safety and security.

12. United Nations Industrial Development Organization (UNIDO):

- Mandate: Promotes industrial development, sustainable production, and technology transfer to enhance economic growth and reduce poverty.

13. World Trade Organization (WTO):

- Mandate: Facilitates trade negotiations, resolves trade disputes, and ensures a rules-based international trading system.

These specialized agencies and programs collaborate with member states and other stakeholders to address global challenges, implement development projects, and promote cooperation in various fields. Each agency has its own governing bodies, leadership, and areas of expertise, contributing to the broader mission of the United Nations to foster international peace, security, and sustainable development.

Collaborative efforts for global challenges

Collaborative efforts for global challenges involve cooperation among countries, international organizations, non-governmental organizations (NGOs), and other stakeholders to address complex and interconnected issues that transcend national boundaries. These challenges include issues such as climate change, poverty, health pandemics, conflict resolution, and more. Collaborative efforts are essential because no single entity or country can effectively address these challenges in isolation. Here are some examples of collaborative efforts for global challenges:

1. Climate Change and Environmental Conservation:

- The Paris Agreement: An international treaty within the United Nations Framework Convention on Climate Change (UNFCCC) where countries commit to reducing greenhouse gas emissions and limiting global warming.
- International Agreements: Collaborative efforts to address issues like deforestation, marine pollution, and endangered species through treaties and conventions.

2. Global Health:

- Vaccine Initiatives: Global partnerships to ensure equitable access to vaccines, such as COVAX for COVID-19 vaccines.
- Disease Eradication: Collaborative efforts to eradicate diseases like polio and malaria through vaccination

campaigns and health interventions.

3. Humanitarian Assistance and Disaster Relief:

- International Red Cross and Red Crescent Movement: Collaborative efforts to provide emergency relief and support to those affected by conflicts and disasters.
- Humanitarian Coalitions: Countries and organizations working together to provide aid and assistance during crises.

4. Peacekeeping and Conflict Resolution:

- United Nations Peacekeeping Missions: Collaborative efforts involving multiple countries to maintain peace and stability in conflict-affected regions.
- Diplomatic Negotiations: International negotiations and mediations to resolve conflicts, such as peace talks and treaties.

5. Poverty Alleviation and Development:

- Sustainable Development Goals (SDGs): A global framework for collaborative efforts to address poverty, inequality, and promote sustainable development.
- International Development Funding: Collaboration to provide financial assistance and development aid to countries in need.

6. Education and Gender Equality:

- Global Education Initiatives: Collaborative efforts to promote access to quality education for all, particularly girls and marginalized groups.
- Gender Equality Advocacy: International campaigns and initiatives to empower women and promote gender equality.

7. Counterterrorism and Security:

- International Counterterrorism Partnerships: Collaborative efforts to combat terrorism through intelligence sharing, law enforcement cooperation, and capacity building.

8. Technological Innovation and Research:

- Collaborative Research: International collaboration in fields like space exploration, medical research, and technology development to address global challenges.

9. Disaster Preparedness and Response:

- Early Warning Systems: International cooperation to develop systems that provide timely warnings for natural disasters and emergencies.
- Disaster Response Teams: Collaborative efforts to provide immediate assistance and relief after disasters.

Collaborative efforts for global challenges require strong international partnerships, effective communication, resource sharing, and a shared commitment to finding solutions. These efforts demonstrate the importance of collective action to tackle issues that impact the well-being of people and the planet on a global scale.

NGOs and their role in policy advocacy

Non-governmental organizations (NGOs) play a crucial role in policy advocacy by representing the interests of communities, individuals, and specific causes to influence decision-making processes at local, national, and international levels. NGOs are independent entities that work outside of government structures, allowing them to provide a diverse range of perspectives and advocate for change on various social, environmental, and humanitarian issues. Here's an overview of the role of NGOs in policy advocacy:

1. Raising Awareness:

- NGOs bring attention to social, environmental, and human rights issues that may not receive sufficient coverage in mainstream media, thereby raising public awareness and concern.

2. Mobilizing Support:

- NGOs mobilize individuals, communities, and stakeholders to support their causes, creating a collective voice that policymakers must take into account.

3. Research and Analysis:

- NGOs conduct research and gather data to provide evidence-based insights and analysis on issues, which can influence policy discussions.

4. Policy Recommendations:

- NGOs propose policy recommendations based on their expertise and research findings, advocating for changes that align with their missions and goals.

5. Lobbying and Advocacy:

- NGOs engage in lobbying efforts by meeting with policymakers, presenting research, and advocating for specific policy changes that reflect their constituents' needs.

6. Grassroots Engagement:

- NGOs often work at the community level, engaging directly with affected populations to amplify their voices and concerns in policy discussions.

7. Legal Advocacy:

- Some NGOs use legal advocacy to challenge policies through litigation or legal action to protect rights, advance justice, and hold governments accountable.

8. Public Campaigns:

- NGOs run public awareness campaigns to rally public support and pressure policymakers to address specific issues.

9. Coalition Building:

- NGOs collaborate with other organizations, forming coalitions that amplify their impact and expand their reach.

10. Monitoring and Accountability:

- NGOs monitor policy implementation, advocating for transparency, accountability, and the fulfillment of commitments.

11. International Advocacy:

- NGOs operate on the international stage, influencing global policies, treaties, and agreements by participating in international forums and conferences.

12. Fill Gaps in Governance:

- NGOs often step in to address gaps in governance, providing services, support, and advocacy in areas where governments may lack resources or capacity.

Challenges and Considerations:

1. **Credibility:** NGOs must maintain credibility by using accurate data and evidence-based research to support their advocacy efforts.
2. **Funding:** NGOs often rely on funding sources, which may impact their independence and priorities.
3. **Representation:** Balancing the diverse perspectives within NGOs and accurately representing the voices of affected communities can be challenging.
4. **Effectiveness:** The impact of NGO advocacy depends on various factors, including the political climate, the issue's urgency, and the level of public support.

NGOs act as a bridge between citizens, communities, and policymakers, advocating for positive change, social justice, and accountability. Their role in policy advocacy helps shape legislation, regulations, and international agreements to address pressing global challenges and advance human rights and well-being.

Humanitarian and development organizations

Humanitarian and development organizations are non-governmental entities that work to address various social, economic, and humanitarian challenges faced by communities and individuals around the world. While both types of organizations aim to improve people's well-being, they often focus on different aspects of assistance and have distinct approaches. Here's an overview of humanitarian and development organizations:

Humanitarian Organizations:

1. **Focus:** Humanitarian organizations primarily respond to emergencies, crises, and disasters, providing immediate relief to save lives and alleviate suffering during and after emergencies.
2. **Objectives:** Their main goal is to provide immediate assistance such as food, clean water, shelter, medical care, and protection to affected populations, especially in conflict zones, natural disasters, and other emergencies.
3. **Approach:** Humanitarian organizations often work in high-risk and challenging environments to deliver rapid and effective assistance, irrespective of long-term development goals.
4. **Examples:** International Committee of the Red Cross (ICRC), Médecins Sans Frontières (Doctors Without Borders), CARE, World Food Programme (WFP).

Development Organizations:

1. **Focus:** Development organizations work on long-term projects aimed at improving the overall quality of life for communities and individuals by addressing underlying structural issues such as poverty, education, healthcare, and economic opportunities.
2. **Objectives:** They strive to build sustainable solutions by focusing on education, healthcare, economic development, infrastructure, gender equality, and other initiatives to uplift communities over the long term.
3. **Approach:** Development organizations often engage in capacity-building, empowering communities to be self-sufficient and resilient, and promoting social and economic progress.
4. **Examples:** United Nations Development Programme (UNDP), Oxfam, World Bank Group, Save the Children.

Collaboration: Humanitarian and development organizations often collaborate, especially in situations where emergencies intersect with ongoing development efforts. For instance, development projects may incorporate disaster preparedness components, and humanitarian response may include efforts to address longer-term development needs.

Challenges and Considerations:

1. **Coordination:** Balancing immediate relief efforts with long-term development initiatives requires careful coordination and collaboration among organizations.
2. **Sustainability:** Both types of organizations must consider how their interventions will have a lasting impact and contribute to sustainable change.
3. **Funding:** Securing funding for both immediate humanitarian relief and longer-term development projects can be challenging due to donor priorities and

resource constraints.

4. **Cultural Sensitivity:** Organizations need to respect local cultures, customs, and preferences while implementing interventions to ensure they are appropriate and effective.
5. **Accountability:** Organizations must be accountable to the communities they serve, donors, and other stakeholders to ensure that resources are used effectively and transparently.

Humanitarian and development organizations play critical roles in addressing global challenges, whether by providing immediate relief in times of crisis or working toward long-term improvements in the well-being of communities and individuals. Their combined efforts contribute to creating a more just and equitable world.

Grassroots activism and social change

Grassroots activism is a powerful approach to initiating social change by mobilizing individuals and communities at the local level to advocate for specific issues, policies, or causes. It involves ordinary people coming together to raise awareness, organize campaigns, and influence decision-makers to address social, political, economic, or environmental concerns. Grassroots activism plays a vital role in promoting democracy, citizen engagement, and positive societal transformation. Here's how grassroots activism contributes to social change:

1. Empowerment of Communities:

- Grassroots activism empowers individuals and communities to take ownership of their concerns and actively participate in the change they want to see.

2. Bottom-Up Approach:

- Grassroots efforts start from the ground level and build momentum as more people join the cause, allowing for a wider range of perspectives and needs to be addressed.

3. Local Relevance:

- Activists understand the specific challenges and needs of their communities, ensuring that efforts and solutions are locally relevant.

4. Creating Awareness:

- Grassroots campaigns raise awareness about issues

that may not receive mainstream attention, giving voice to marginalized and underserved populations.

5. Advocacy and Mobilization:

- Grassroots activists organize rallies, protests, letter-writing campaigns, and petitions to put pressure on policymakers and decision-makers to take action.

6. Building Alliances:

- Grassroots efforts often lead to alliances with other organizations, forming a broader coalition that increases collective impact.

7. Policy Change:

- Grassroots activism can influence policy changes at local, national, and international levels by putting pressure on legislators and officials.

8. Social Norm Shift:

- Grassroots movements challenge societal norms, promoting inclusivity, equality, and justice.

9. Addressing Systemic Issues:

- Grassroots activism can highlight systemic injustices and inequalities that require fundamental changes in policies, institutions, and structures.

10. Long-Term Impact:

- Grassroots activism aims for sustained change over time, focusing on creating lasting shifts in attitudes, policies, and behaviors.

Challenges and Considerations:

1. **Resources:** Grassroots activists may face challenges in terms of funding, time, and expertise to effectively

organize and sustain campaigns.

2. **Resistance:** Powerful interests or authorities may resist grassroots efforts, leading to obstacles and potential backlash.
3. **Visibility:** Gaining visibility and media coverage can be difficult for grassroots campaigns, as mainstream media often prioritize sensational stories.
4. **Sustainability:** Maintaining momentum and engagement over the long term requires sustained effort and community involvement.
5. **Diverse Voices:** Ensuring diverse representation and inclusion within grassroots movements can be a challenge but is essential for addressing various perspectives.

Grassroots activism has historically played a significant role in social change movements, from civil rights to environmental justice. By engaging communities and individuals in meaningful ways, grassroots efforts create a collective force for change and inspire broader societal transformations that lead to a more just and equitable world.